TABLE OF CONTENTS

- I. INTRODUCTION 1
  - A. MAJOR RESEARCH QUESTION 1
  - B. IMPORTANCE 2
  - C. PROBLEMS AND HYPOTHESES 3
  - D. LITERATURE REVIEW 5
  - E. METHODS AND SOURCES 9
  - F. THESIS OVERVIEW 10
- II. WHY DOES STRATEGIC PARTNERSHIP BETWEEN NATO AND RUSSIA MATTER? 11
  - A. CONVERGING INTERESTS AND DIVERSIFYING CHALLENGES IN A NEW SECURITY ENVIRONMENT 11
  - B. THE RUSSIAN PERSPECTIVE 15
  - C. NATO'S PERSPECTIVE 21
- III. GEOPOLITICS OF RUSSIA, DISTINCT RUSSIAN IDENTITY, AND THEIR IMPLICATIONS ON FOREIGN-POLICY DECISIONS OF MOSCOW 27
  - A. GEOGRAPHY AND GEOPOLITICS 27
  - B. RUSSIAN IDENTITY 34
  - C. ANTI-WESTERN SENTIMENT? 39
  - D. CONTESTING IDEOLOGIES 44
  - E. RELIGION 50
  - F. CONCLUSION 53
- IV. VLADIMIR PUTIN AND RUSSIAN FOREIGN POLICY IN THE TWENTY-FIRST CENTURY 55
  - A. RUSSIA'S ASSERTIVE FOREIGN POLICY IN THE TWENTY-FIRST CENTURY 55
    1. Internal Factors 56
    2. External Factors 59
  - B. IS PUTIN ANTI-WESTERN? 61
    1. The Presidency's Influence in the Making of Foreign Policy 62
    2. The Putin Administration 63
    3. Putin's Third Term 66
- V. COOPERATIVE SECURITY AND THE NATO-RUSSIA RELATIONS 69
  - A. COLLECTIVE DEFENSE, COLLECTIVE SECURITY, AND COOPERATIVE SECURITY 69
  - B. COOPERATIVE SECURITY AND NATO- RUSSIAN RELATIONS ...73
  - C. THE LATE COLD WAR ERA 75
  - D. THE POST–COLD WAR ERA 77
  - E. POST–SEPTEMBER 11 ERA 83
  - F. CONCLUSION 86

i

VI.	**CONCLUSION**	**89**
	LIST OF REFERENCES	**95**

LIST OF ACRONYMS AND ABBREVIATIONS

CIS	Commonwealth of Independent States
CFE	Conventional Forces in Europe
EU	European Union
NAC	North Atlantic Council
NACC	North Atlantic Cooperation Council
NATO	North Atlantic Treaty Organization
NRC	NATO-Russia Council
OSCE	Organization for Security and Cooperation in Europe
PfP	Partnership for Peace
PJC	Permanent Joint Council
USSR	Union of Soviet Socialist Republics
WMD	Weapon of Mass Destruction

THIS PAGE INTENTIONALLY LEFT BLANK

I. INTRODUCTION

A. MAJOR RESEARCH QUESTION

Many critics of NATO alert to its relations to Russia often doubt it efficacy as a security organization, while ignoring its remarkable transformation since 1989. "With the end of the Cold War, North Atlantic Treaty Organization (NATO) has continued to struggle to define its identity and clarify its raison d'etre."[1] Russia, in the meanwhile, has sought to overcome its economic and political imbalances and promote its assertiveness in both its traditional sphere of influence and the international stage. Relations between the two entities oscillated between excessive optimism and over-pessimism on the common denominator of distrust. This study aims to answer the question of whether a common ground of international relations and security could be constructed between NATO and Russia by analyzing all impeding factors, shared interests, and common challenges that could serve as an inhibitor or catalyst in promoting a strategic partnership.

The thesis aims also to understand NATO and Russian security perceptions and foreign and security policies towards each other and to scrutinize the prospects of achieving a healthy partnership in the areas of security and defense. In this connection, the analysis treats the following questions: How relations between Russia and NATO evolved at the turn of the 21st century, and whether constructive initiatives of NATO, under its cooperative security approach, would help overcome difficulties and obstacles in normalizing relations and promoting a strategic partnership between the two former enemies. Ultimately, the thesis seeks to answer the broad question of whether it is possible for Russia and NATO to make a clean sweep of lingering legacies of deep-seated antagonism and distrust, move beyond cultural, religious, and historical differences, and lay the foundations of a healthy lasting partnership.

---

[1] Aurel Braun, NATO-Russia Relations in the Twenty-First Century, New York, NY: Routledge, 2008, 1.

B. **IMPORTANCE**

NATO–Russian relations constitute one of the major components of the 21st century's new security architecture in the Euro-Atlantic region, especially for those who regard the fate of Europe and its adjoining areas key to world peace. The new security environment of post-September 11 has prepared a common ground for a closer partnership between old enemies. However, the attempts from both sides have been unable to move beyond a certain level of cooperation. This thesis will seek to illuminate the importance and possibility of the NATO–Russia strategic partnership under the 21st century's new security considerations by analyzing the common interests, concerns, and expectations of the parties and the origins of the friction in the light of key events and developments in the last two decades.

Since the end of Cold War, NATO has sought to justify its existence and make its raison d'etre clear. It pursued an eastward enlargement, integrating most of the former Commonwealth of Independent States (CIS) countries and sought to create a stable space suitable for democracy, rule of law, human rights, and market economy to flourish, while trying to avoid any confrontation with Russia. Russia usually considered NATO's enlargement as a threat to its national security and interests. The relations of NATO and Russia have progressed on a rocky path during the two decades following the fall of the Berlin Wall, oscillating between the promise of stronger partnership in an era of unpredictable, asymmetric, transnational threats to global security, and lingering memories of old antagonism and distrust.

"Russia [always] remained a major factor in Allied calculations."[2] Despite its collapsed economy and heavily weakened military, Russia has maintained its potential for enhancing its economic growth and revitalizing its strategic significance as a nuclear power and a natural-resource-rich country.[3] NATO and the United States still possess

---

[2] Stanley R. Sloan, Permanent Alliance? NATO and the Transatlantic Bargain from Truman to Obama, New York, NY: Continuum, 2010, 130.

[3] Ibid., 130.

ninety percent of world's nuclear arsenal.[4] Furthermore, Lionel Ponsard asserts that "NATO's future not only depended on its ability to adapt to new international environment, but it was closely related to the turn of its future relations with Russian Federation."[5] Aware of this reality, NATO pursued a constructive attitude towards Russia and sought to avoid any serious confrontation.

This research is pertinent due to the vital role of Russian–NATO relations for the future of both the West and Russia. Given the more complex threats to global security today, the rising energy demand and dependency of Europe, and increasing foreign trade between the parties, Russia's relations with the West, as a major fossil-fuel exporter and nuclear country, have become increasingly important.

C. PROBLEMS AND HYPOTHESES

This thesis examines whether two former enemies of the cold war, NATO and Russia, could further their cooperation to the level of a true strategic partnership in the 21st century. It analyzes the factors increasing or decreasing this possibility, the evolution of the NATO–Russia relationship in the last two decades, and how the cooperative-security concept has worked in this process. Lionel Ponsard argues, "There is still a long way to go before these relations will be fully normalized. However, this past decade of oscillating relations is very instructive in many respects."[6]

Many scholars object to the idea of integration of Russia into the alliance and West on the grounds that it has a distinct identity and belongs to Asia, and may cause the alliance to collapse from within; while some assert that Russia's progress towards democracy and Western values since Peter the Great was interrupted by the Bolshevik Revolution and that the collapse of Soviet Union has enabled parties to resume, and even hasten, this progress. This thesis seeks to illuminate commonalities and differences between Russia and West in terms of values, norms, and institutions. It tries to answer

---

[4] NATO Secretary General Anders Fogh Rasmussen speech at the University of Chicago's Harris School, 12 May 2012, http://www.natochannel.tv/?uri=channels/381662/1332785

[5] Lionel Ponsard, Russia, NATO and cooperative Security: Bridging the Gap, London and New York, NY: Routledge, 2007, 1.

[6] Ibid., 2.

whether and how they can leave the unpleasant legacies of fifty years behind and move forward to a smoother course of relations. The Russian identity and political culture will be analyzed and the impact of Putin's administration will be analyzed.

The new threat perceptions and security system introduced by the terrorist attacks in September 11, 2001 have necessitated closer cooperation and partnership globally. "The new threats to world security are defined as unpredictable, transnational, asymmetric, and nonconventional."[7] In this new context, this study seeks to illuminate the common challenges and interests of the two former enemies that bring them together in an era of uncertainty. It discusses the perspectives of Brussels and Moscow by analyzing their expectations and concerns under the light of important events and developments in the past two decades.

Overall, this thesis examines the hypothesis that, despite many risks and obstacles, improvement of relations and achievement of a stronger cooperation and strategic partnership is still possible and important in the NATO–Russia relations, and requires only positive approaches from the two entities. There are many opportunities for rebuilding trust and strengthening relations, as well as many impediments. The parties need to concentrate on opportunities and commonalities rather than over-focusing on obstacles and differences, if they are to promote peace and stability in Europe. NATO needs to acknowledge that Russia evolves differently and should remain patient as Russian journeys to democracy and predictability. It also has to be ready to recognize a greater say for Russia in its designs for frictionless, sustainable relations and a stable and peace-promoting Europe. Russia, on the other hand, should put aside old hatreds, limit its ambitions, and grasp how costly it could be for it to deepen the cleavages. Lionel Ponsard argues that "by building confidence between the two parties about each other's intentions, cooperative security can regulate attitudes that might otherwise lead to misperception."[8] In this sense, the NATO–Russia Council (NRC) can serve as a dialogue medium, which is crucial for elimination of biases, concern, and misperceptions.

---

[7] Ibid., 2.
[8] Ibid., 3.

D. **LITERATURE REVIEW**

In conducting research for this thesis, sources of various types were consulted. These include works examining perspectives on Russia and NATO and Russia's political institutions, culture, foreign policy, and compatibility with Western values. The works below were drawn upon frequently and helped support to arguments of the thesis.

Aurel Braun's editorial work *NATO–Russia Relations in the Twenty-First Century* is a collection of articles regarding the NATO–Russia relations. This study examines first the internal and external dynamics that influence these relations. It provides a theoretical framework for Russia's transition to democracy, which is seen by many as the biggest hampering factor in the NATO–Russia relations, and analyzes the impact of NATO's policies on relations, providing both optimistic and pessimistic views, according to the various scholars. Aurel Braun asserts, "As the Alliance also sought simultaneously to enhance its cooperation with Russia, the latter has become more assertive just as its transition to democracy has become more uncertain. Yet all parties have a powerful interest in building and maintaining security."[9] He concludes that both sides need a realistic perspective that is aware of both opportunities and obstacles in the 21st century. And he highlights that "there is consensus among the contributors that, although there are opportunities for building trust and strengthening democracies in a new NATO–Russia relationship in this century, there are also many risks and grave dangers."[10]

Lionel Ponsard's book *Russia, NATO and Cooperative Security* explores the common ground between NATO and Russia and the potential to move beyond cultural differences, particularly in political culture.[11] It aims to find out if cooperative security could be helpful in this regard and concludes affirmatively. He asserts "the closer the interaction between NATO and Russia, the more they will find ways to further their security and understanding one another."[12] He believes history is very helpful for extracting lessons that can be applied to further interactions, and if NATO and Russia

---

[9] Braun, *NATO–Russia Relations in the Twenty-First Century*, 1.

[10] Ibid., 7.

[11] Ponsard, *Bridging the Gap*, Introduction, 1.

[12] Ibid., 3.

make a clean sweep of mutual distrust and draw appropriate lessons from the past, it is highly possible for them to construct a true strategic partnership in the future.

Stanley R. Sloan asserts in his work *'Permanent Alliance?'* that in the post–Cold War global order, NATO's primary concern has moved beyond Russia. However, it has remained a major factor, as it still is a nuclear power and and has the potential of making a big economic leap with its natural-resource-rich territory, even if its economy and military collapsed.[13] He emphasizes the clash of domination over Central and Eastern Europe over the former CIS countries. He asserts that the Russian domestic political atmosphere is the most important variable of mutual relations. The anti-democratic and authoritarian tendencies of Russian political leadership have negative consequences for relations. He asserts that

> . . . NATO faces a true dilemma: cooperation with Russia is a key element of future European and international peace; but NATO's integrity requires that the values for which the alliance stands—democracy, individual liberty, and the rule of law—and the interests of the allies in defending their security remain at the heart of the alliance's purpose."[14] Therefore, NATO countries design their policies around constructive involvement of Russia in European and global security affairs, aware of " . . . European security cannot be confidently secured without Moscow's constructive participation.[15]

The work of Kjell Engelbrekt and Bertyl Nygren, *Russia and Europe: Building Bridges, Digging Trenches*, collects many related articles under three main topics. Their study aims to shed light on the relations of Russia with the West and the possibility of its integration into Europe. The first part examines Russian norms, values, and institutions, in addition to the Russian way of democracy. The question of where Russia belongs is examined in this chapter.

Trofimenko concludes that "there is an 'emerging consensus' that Russia 'has to follow its own unique ways and traditions because Russia is neither a purely Western nor purely Eastern nation, but blends in its nature a combination of both cultures, psches, and

---

[13] Sloan, Permanent Alliance, 130.

[14] Ibid.,143.

[15] Ibid., 144.

even genes."[16] Ideational and cultural differences, Nygren asserts, constitute the main factors in the friction between the West and Russia. The second part analyzes Moscow's relations with Brussels and three European great powers, focusing on hard security and economic dimensions. They argue that the worldwide economic recession has undermined Russia's authoritarian political leadership's authority and legitimacy, which was strenghtened by the economic growth achieved during the first decade of the 21st century. This may render amelioration of relations possible on the grounds that, as he believes, the Putin administration is one of the major impediments to relations. On the other hand, he asserts that "NATO will be considered a threat unless, it is granted a genuine say in the organization (or even membership) and NATO seriously downplays its article five orientation."[17] In the third part of his work, Trofimenko examines the influence of the conflict of West and Russia over the former Soviet republics and former communist countries of Eastern and Central Europe.

Stephen K. Wegren and Dale R. Herspring's book, *After Putin's Russia,* examines the Putin administration's impact on domestic political culture, economy, society, military, and foreign policy in Russia. It is helpful in understanding the internal political dynamics of Russia and its reflections in foreign policy. It also shed light on the present situation in Russia in terms of democracy, freedoms, and individual liberties.

Michael McFaul, Nikolai Petrov, and Andrei Ryabov's book *Between Democracy and Dictatorship,* a collection of articles regarding the Russian political system in the post–Cold War era, seeks to answer the question of how democracy evolved after the fall of communism in Russia and what factors contributed to this process. They basically argue that Russia is not a full democracy, but not a dictatorship either. Beyond simplistic and optimistic approaches, their study provides a deep and realistic view of the current situation in Russian political life.

---

[16] Tormifenko, Russian National Interests and the Current Crisis in Russia,187–88 in Kjell Engelbrekt, and Bertil Nygren: Russia and Europe: Building Bridges, Digging Trenches, New York, NY: Routledge, 2010, 4.

[17] Kjell Engelbrekt, and Bertil Nygren: *Russia and Europe: Building Bridges, Digging Trenches,* New York, NY: Routledge, 2010, 8.

David Yost examines the evolution of NATO's assumed roles during the Cold War and its aftermath in his work *NATO Transformed*. He assesses the alliance's post–Cold War policies and institutions and asserts that "NATO's self-assigned new role as an 'agent of change' throughout Europe has raised great challenges, as well as questions about the future purposes and nature of the alliance."[18] Due to the open-ended enlargement process, NATO has had to face many challenges that could threaten the peace and stability of Europe. Russia has claimed that enlargement of NATO undermines its security and objected to NATO's attempts to enlarge the process. Yost claims, in this regard, that "no issue is more central to the Alliance's goal of a building a peaceful political order in Europe than relations with Russia,"[19] and examines NATO–Russian relations beginning from NACC to Founding Act and PJC.

Jeffrey Mankoff's work *Russian Foreign Policy: The Return of Great Power Politics* explores the components of Russian foreign policy and the factors that shape it. He basically argues that Russia is neither anti- nor pro-Western, but rather, pragmatic. He analyzes the ideological and political currents in Russia that are reconciled in the style of Vladimir Putin. He also examines the relations between the West and Russia and explores the prospects of confrontation and integration. He draws particular attention to the geopolitical dynamism around Russia by pointing China's rise. And he finally analyzes the course of Russian foreign policy's outlook since the breakup of the Soviet Union.

Robert H. Donaldson and Joseph L. Nogee attempt in their book *The Foreign Policy of Russia: Changing Systems, Enduring Interests to* present a description and an explanation of Russian foreign policy. They frame their study in a historical context by covering the late Soviet era and the 20th century, and explore the tsarist and Soviet legacies in the current foreign policy of Moscow. While exploring internal and external factors, they bring continuities and changes in dynamic to the attention of the reader.

---

[18] David S. Yost, *NATO Transformed: The Alliance's New Roles in International Security*, Washington, D.C.: United States Institute of Peace Press, 1998, 91.

[19] Ibid., 131.

They basically argue that Russian foreign policy has not been different from that of other great powers, even though it has had some unique aspects.

Ian Q.R. Thomas' work *The Promise of Alliance: NATO and the Political Imagination* explores conceptions of NATO's form and function and the changes in NATO's goals and objectives since its creation in 1949 and throughout the Cold War and aftermath. Thomas argues that those who believe that NATO sooner or later will be defunct with the end of the Cold War are mistaken, since NATO's record is remarkable in perpetuating itself through new rhetoric and conception that reflect initiatives of collective defense and cooperative security of notable merit, despite all detractors assertions to the contrary.

E. METHODS AND SOURCES

This thesis is based on a qualitative historical study and analysis that includes the critical analyses of variables affecting the NATO–Russia relations. First, It will examine the historical, structural, and political components of these variables through an analytical method. It will also include a comparative assessment of Russian and NATO perspectives and their impact on contemporary and future relations. The evolution of the NATO–Russia relations will be put in historical perspective, and continuities and discontinuities in relations will be explored. In the final part of the thesis, the relations between two entities will be assessed in the context of the cooperative-security concept. How a constructivist approach is helpful for the wellbeing of relations, as compared with a realist approach, will be explained by a comparative method.

This thesis relies on both primary and secondary resources. NATO's 1991, 1999, and 2010 strategic concepts and Russia's new strategic concept and military doctrine (2010) will be evaluated within the context of the NATO–Russia relations. The North Atlantic Treaty, Founding Act (1997), and remarks and statements of leaders, summit communiqués of NATO, NATO–Russia Council meeting declarations, official documents, press conferences and releases will be used as primary sources, in addition to the sources in the literature review.

F. THESIS OVERVIEW

The thesis is organized as follows: Chapter II explores why partnership is necessary and important. The post–September 11 security environment and common interests of Russia and NATO are analyzed in this chapter. A comparison of Russian and NATO perspectives is also presented.

Chapter III examines the sources of friction between Russia and NATO. It aims to unveil the political, cultural, and geographical factors that distance Russia from West.

Chapter IV analyzes Russian foreign policy in the 21st century and attempts to explain to what extent Vladimir Putin has been influential.

Chapter V analyzes the importance of the cooperative-security concept and constructive efforts of parties in the post–Cold War era. How much these initiatives, from NACC to NRC, have been helpful is evaluated.

II. WHY DOES STRATEGIC PARTNERSHIP BETWEEN NATO AND RUSSIA MATTER?

This chapter analyzes the transformation in the security environment in the 21st century and the needs and roles of international political actors in an era of rapid change. Next, it presents the need for cooperation and partnership between NATO and Russia, by analyzing shared interests and common challenges; finally, the perspectives of involved parties and their concerns, expectations, and latest strategy documents are assessed.

A. CONVERGING INTERESTS AND DIVERSIFYING CHALLENGES IN A NEW SECURITY ENVIRONMENT

Since the breakup of the Soviet Union and end of the Cold War, the security environment and threats to the security of countries, alliances, and the entire world have changed dramatically. Technological and geopolitical changes have revolutionized threat perceptions and means of assuring security. The relatively stagnant and predictable nature of the Cold War has been replaced by unprecedented uncertainty and unpredictability. Regional ethnic and religious conflicts in the Balkans, Caucasus, Middle East, Central Asia, Africa, and South Asia, and the emergence of transnational terrorist organizations, religious radicalization, shifts in global economic balances, the proliferation of weapons of mass destruction (WMD) and nuclear weapons, and rising demand for energy and water supplies pose great risks to global security and peace by the atmosphere of uncertainty and unpredictability they have created. Among the increasing imbalances, states seek security either by increasing their defense spending, and accordingly their military power, or making alliances through which to pool their capabilities.

The changing balance in today's geopolitical setting from unipolarity to multipolarity is one of the major concerns of the era. The demographic and economic rise of the East and South Asia and the awakening of the Muslim world complicate the strategic calculations of the older great powers. Two main actors of the Cold War era, Russia—the heir of the Soviet Union—and the U.S. and its NATO allies have devoted significant attention and effort to reading this change and lessening uncertainty. As a component of global security, Euro-Atlantic security, in which Russia and NATO are the major actors, suffers the same problems and is threatened by similar realities. The peace and stability in the Euro-Atlantic, which has been threatened by numerous ethnic and religious conflicts, mushrooming radical Islamic groups and terrorist organizations, cyber-terrorism, energy insecurity, the increasing illegal drug trade, and organized crime, necessitates cooperation and common efforts among all countries, particularly Russia and NATO. However, Russia and NATO have failed to carry their relationship to a strategic level, despite the road they have covered. The former UK ambassador to Russia, Andrew Wood, notes that if Euro-Atlantic actors and Russia are to address the challenges and threats of the 21st century, they have to set the NATO–Russia relationship on a unambiguous course. [20] Considering how far Russia and NATO have come in their relations since the height of the Cold War, a sound relationship is not a wishful thinking, but rather an achievable goal.

A quick glance at the key events in the first decade of the 21st century reveals the enormous changes that have occurred in the security environment and threat perceptions and security policies of Russia and NATO countries:

- The terrorist attacks of 11 September 2001, followed by NATO's operations in Afghanistan and Iraq
- The attacks by Islamic terrorists in Madrid and London metros in 2004 and 2005
- NATO enlargements in 1999, 2004 and 2009
- The cyber attack on Estonian servers in 2007 that crashed the country's public-communications infrastructure
- The enormous increase in piracy in the Gulf of Aden, one of the most important maritime trade routes in the world.
- The resurgence of the political goal of a nuclear-free world, suggested by U.S President Barack Obama in Prague in 2009.
- Reform of the European Union (EU) through the Lisbon Treaty in 2009, which anchored a solidarity and mutual assistance clause in the and thereby laid the foundations for a European Defense Union
- The Arab Spring in Tunisia and Algeria in December 2010

---

[20] Andrew Wood, "*A Joint Review of the Challenges and Threats of the 21st Century*," in Indivisibility of Security: Russia and Euro-Atlantic Security, ed. Andrew Monaghan Forum Paper No.13, 86–96, NATO Defense College, January 2010.

- NATO's intervention in Libya in March 2011 followed by the overthrow and death of Muammar Gaddafi.
- Ongoing conflicts in Syria since March 2011.[21]

This short list of events that occurred in the past decade reveals the complexity of the security environment and the necessity of dialogue, cooperation, and partnership among countries and organizations, particularly NATO and Russia.

In the 2010 Strategic Concept of NATO, proliferation of nuclear weapons and WMDs and international terrorism are perceived as major threats, along with more conventional threats. They cause significant concern in the alliance because of the danger they pose to global stability and prosperity. Among new phenomena in the 21st century, terrorism is perceived as a direct threat to the NATO countries and global security. The increasing probability of terrorist group's acquisition of nuclear, biological, chemical, and radiological weapons aggravates the problem. In addition to those three main threats, cyber attacks, piracy, overdependence on energy imports, environmental problems, and resource constrains, including climate change, water scarcity, and health risks, pose increasing threats and risks to global security and NATO's interests.[22]

2010 Strategic Concept also draws attention to the importance of developing relations between NATO and Russia, which is essential for the creation of a common space of peace, stability, and security. It also suggests a need for the improvement of partnership to a true strategic level. Despite differences on particular issues, it acknowledges that the security of NATO and Russia are intertwined.[23] To this end, "At Lisbon, the 29 the NATO–Russia Council (NRC) leaders . . . endorsed [also] a joint review of 21st century common security challenges, which include Afghanistan, terrorism, piracy, the proliferation of weapons of mass destruction and their means of delivery, and natural and man-made disasters."[24] Andrew Monaghan, a research advisor

---

[21] Christos Katsioulis, *"The New NATO Strategy: A Temporary Compromise,"* International Policy Analysis, Friedrich Ebert Foundation, January 2011.

[22] North Atlantic Council, Strategic Concept, 20 November 2010, par. 7–15.

[23] Ibid., par. 33.

[24] *"NATO's relations with Russia,"* NATO Official Webpage, http://www nato.int/cps/en/natolive/topics_50090.htm

at the NATO Defense College, suggests, "In effect, this review has a dual purpose. First, it underscores the attempt to change perceptions—stating that NATO and Russia share common interests and face common challenges. Second, it hones the NATO–Russia agenda by identifying a range of cooperation projects."[25]

Most recently, at the Chicago Summit in May 2012, the importance of the NATO–Russia cooperation in the face of the challenges and threats of the 21st century was underlined as follows:

> NATO–Russia cooperation is of strategic importance as it contributes to creating a common space of peace, stability and security. We remain determined to build a lasting and inclusive peace, together with Russia, in the Euro-Atlantic area, based upon the goals, principles and commitments of the NATO–Russia Founding Act and the Rome Declaration. We want to see a true strategic partnership between NATO and Russia, and we will act accordingly with the expectation of reciprocity from Russia.[26]

In the Chicago Summit declaration, the importance of the role of the NRC as a forum for transparent political dialogue was emphasized. Particularly, at a practical level, cooperation in Afghanistan with regard to transit arrangements, training of narcotics personnel, helicopter maintenance, and counterterrorism cooperation and exercise was indicated as the sign of a common determination to build peace and stability in the region.

From the standpoint of Moscow, the preservation of stability and peace in Europe is as important as a goal of policy. Russia's economic and social recovery requires preservation of the international status quo. Furthermore, geopolitical dynamism around Russia itself compels Russia to have a stable Western border, that is to say, good relations and cooperation. The threats perceived by NATO's 2010 Strategic Concept are entirely relevant to Moscow. Moscow's dealing with them individually is unthinkable, considering the complexity and, particularly, transnational character of some of them.

---

[25] Andrew Monaghan, *"From Lisbon to Munich: Russian Views of NATO–Russia Relations,"* Research Report, NATO Defense College, February 2011. http://www.ndc.nato.int/research/series.php?icode=3

[26] North Atlantic Council, Chicago Summit Declaration, 20 May 2012, Par. 36.

B. **THE RUSSIAN PERSPECTIVE**

"Geopolitics argues that it is geography which defines power, and that military and economic and political power are different parts of a single system."[27] We need to look briefly at Russia's geopolitical conditions to be able to make an assessment regarding its perspective on NATO. Russia has been experiencing structural economic problems, a demographic decline, and a military undergoing a transformation while having to deal with insurgency in the northern Caucasus. The global economic crisis slows down Moscow and reduces policy effectiveness in addressing those issues. Therefore, "Foreign policy under both Putin and Medvedev has been aimed at creating a favorable environment for economic and sociopolitical modernization, while ensuring that Russia is not weakened on the international scene."[28] Still, because of its vast geographical size, abundance of natural resources, and nuclear capabilities, Russia continues to be a power, despite enduring demographic, military, and economic problems. However, all things considered, including emerging dynamic geopolitical actors around its borders, these challenges compel Russia into closer partnership with NATO.

The challenges Russia is facing in the 21st century are listed and described in such security and strategy documents as *Foreign Policy Concept, National Strategy Document* and *Military Doctrine* (MD). The concern over NATO's enlargement of its borders and influence into close proximity with Russia's borders, and installments of missile defense units in Central and Eastern Europe, are common themes in these documents. Particularly, MD still refers to NATO as a "military danger," if not anymore a "threat." On the other hand, these documents without exception stress on the need for closer relations, cooperation, and partnership with NATO. This ambivalence actually can be read as the desire of Russia for partnership and cooperation, despite its lack of trust.

---

[27] George Friedman, "*The World in the Next 100 Years,*" 27 August 2009, http://www.newstatesman.com/north-america/2009/08/power-china-world-japan-poland, accessed on 6 November 2012.

[28] Isabelle François, "*The United States, Russia, Europe, and Security: How to Address the Unfinished Business of the Post–Cold War Era*" Center for Transatlantic Security Studies, Institute for National Strategic Studies, NATO Defense University, April 2012 http://www.ndu.edu/inss/docuploaded/CTSS%20Transatlantic%20Perspectives%202.pdf

The resolved and unresolved conflicts within and around the borders of Russia have substantial impact in its strategic thinking. Russia has the biggest territorial space and longest land borders in the world. Since the breakup of the Soviet Union, many border disputes with China and Japan remain unresolved. There are troubled areas as Transnistria, Abkhazia, South Ossetia, Nagorno-Karabakh, and Chechenistan that bear a high potential of reappearing conflict. Particularly, the conflict over Russian forces in Chechnya troubled much of the post-Soviet era. Including that in the arctic, current and potential territorial claims and the frozen conflicts in the former Soviet space have great effect on Russian strategic thinking. [29]

Another major issue affecting traditional Russian thinking is the geopolitical dynamism and ongoing change in the security environment around Russia. The growing influence of NATO and the EU in the West, emerging economic and political influence of China in the Southeast, and the rise of Islamic fundamentalism in the South have forced Russia to reconsider its geopolitical priorities and national strategies. Furthermore, Moscow's loss of strategic ground and influence in Central Asia, the South Caucasus, and Central and Eastern Europe have aggravated its strategic position and made its deep-seated insecurity even worse. Russian leaders has remained skeptical, particularly, in relations with Western countries and security organizations, which they blame for taking advantage of Russia's temporary weakness in the immediate aftermath of the collapse of the Soviet Union.[30]

Vis-à-vis China, a growing concern of Russian policymakers cannot be overlooked, despite seemingly good relations and close cooperation and partnership between Moscow and Beijing. Russia considers its partnership and cooperation with China as a big gain; however, it remains ambivalent about the future of the relationship and does not want to become a junior partner of its rising neighbor.[31]

---

[29] Dmitri Trenin *"Russia's Threat Perception and Strategic Posture,"* in Russian Security Strategy under Putin: U.S. and Russian Perspectives, Strategic Studies Institute, U.S. Army War College, November 2007. Accessed September 16, 2012, http://www.strategicstudiesinstitute.army mil/pdffiles/pub829.pdf.

[30] Ibid.

[31] Ibid.

Principally, Moscow sees the United States and NATO as strategic competitors and is concerned about their military and political presence near Russian borders. Moscow does not want to engage in a submissive relationship with them either. Moscow seeks equality in its relationships with all other political entities, whether it is NATO and the U.S. or China. As Dmitri Trenin, the deputy director of the Carnegie Moscow Center and chair of its foreign and security policy program, notes, "Rather than being sandwiched between two superpowers, Russia hopes to be a major independent actor and maybe even an arbiter between the two."[32]

All these territorial disputes, conflicts, and the geopolitical dynamism around Russia's periphery have reinforced Moscow's deep-seated sense of insecurity and shaped its strategic priorities in the 21st century. In the middle of such geopolitical dynamism and potential conflicts, Russia has tried to bolster its strategic deterrence and military capabilities. It has been modernizing its military and investing in space and satellite systems and nuclear and cyber technology for a decade. All things considered, given the growing instability and dynamic threats around its borders and potential conflicts in former Soviet space, it is best for Russia's interest to have a peaceful and stable European space to its west. Russia has no other option but to repair and consolidate its relations with the West. Nobody can argue that a Russian–U.S. or NATO alliance against China in the future is impossible or irrelevant.

Even though Russian strategic policymakers value Machtpolitik and prioritize power, notably military power, over every other foreign-policy tool, their awareness regarding the economic and cultural means for exerting political influence is increasing. In this sense, they are in favor of maintaining and improving stability in Europe. Hence, Moscow, principally, is happy with the overall course of the relations with the EU and NATO that has allowed Russia increasing, if not completely, equal say since the establishment of North Atlantic Cooperation Council (NACC) in December 1991.

---

[32] Ibid.

Russian policies, therefore, are not anti-American or anti-anything, Moscow is open to any relationship, cooperation or partnership that fits within its interests and is based on the principle of equality.

It is true that there are some milieus in Moscow that see NATO particularly as a threat, blaming it for being an imperialist political and military instrument of the U.S. and causing the difficulties Russia has been experiencing in the Northern Caucasus and other former Soviet areas.[33] Those cadres, most of which are conservative and nationalist forces that dominate the defense and security institutions, claim that NATO's real target is still Russia and the rhetoric regarding terrorism, sea piracy, narcotics, or cyber attacks is a sham.[34] Michael Bohm, the opinion editor of the Moscow Times, claims, "This fear was reflected in Russia's latest military strategy, published in February [2012], in which NATO was listed as the country's No.1 danger." To them, called by some *Slavophiles*, Russian membership is not a good idea for two reasons: first, it brings Russia to a status of another large European Country that would mean giving up its sovereignty and independence, and particularly its global great-power dreams; and second, Russia would become subordinate to the U.S. within this organization.[35] Even though the Putin administration is not anti-Western, its concerns regarding sovereignty and independence in foreign policy and the economy, and conditions and reservations regarding equality in relationships, are reflections of the views of this influential group within the security and defense organizations.

Lately, after the Obama's "reset" initiative, Russia-NATO relationship entered a new phase despite the persistence of distrust between parties. "Russia's ambassador to NATO, Dmitry Rogozin, echoed such views, observing that the relationship had improved and entered a qualitatively new level."[36] It is important to state that Medvedev's acknowledgement of the necessity of participation by all parties in a sound

---

[33] Wood, "*Joint Review of the Challenges and Threats.*"

[34] "Michael Bohm , "*5 Reasons Why Russia Will Never Join NATO,*" The Moscow Times, November 19, 2010, accessed September 16, 2012. http://www.themoscowtimes.com/opinion/article/5-reasons-why-russia-will-never-join-nato/423840.html

[35] Ibid.

[36] Monaghan, "*From Lisbon to Munich.*"

and healthy Euro-Atlantic security is determinative. As Medvedev, then president said, security is indivisible, referring to the concept of "indivisibility of security," and everybody has its part to play in protecting it. No country can achieve it alone.[37]

With regard to the 'indivisibility of security', Sergei Lavrov, currently Foreign Minister of Russia, claims, "This principle [indivisibility of security] was proclaimed by OSCE, NATO and the NATO–Russia Council (NRC) alike. But whereas the North Atlantic Alliance made indivisible security a legally binding norm, the OSCE and the NRC have not gone beyond mere political declarations, lacking any legal or practical content."[38] He goes on to say, "We would like the NRC proclaimed principles of indivisibility of security in Europe to be translated into practice."[39]

Two things are obvious in both of these speeches and the NATO-Russia relations on the whole: first the lack of mutual trust—Moscow is skeptical about the words and deeds of NATO; second, Russia's desire to cooperate, integrate; or being treated on equal terms. Moscow still views itself on the periphery of NATO's decision-making and planning due, to three reasons that reinforces its distrust against NATO. First, it considers that NATO is ambivalent about Russia and sees it both a partner and a potential threat; second the NRC in practice retains a "28+1" format that leaves it out of the actual decision-shaping function; and third, Moscow's proposals are ignored or rejected. NATO's potential global roles can harm Russian interests; such practical policy issues as enlargement and missile defense and NATO's fading influence in international relations are other factors contributing to Russian decision makers' ambivalence. At an operational level, the view regarding NATO's global posture and interests tends to predominate; at a more strategic level, however, NATO's fading influence causes more concern, if membership becomes a consideration.[40]

---

[37] Wood, *"Joint Review of the Challenges and Threats."*

[38] Sergey V. Lavrov, *"Euro-Atlantic: Equal Security for All,"* Official Site of The Ministry of Foreign Affairs of the Russian Federation, 24 May 2010,
http://www mid ru/brp 4 nsf/0/EF1F3C48AD0E5959C325772D0041FA53.

[39] Monaghan, *"From Lisbon to Munich."*

[40] Ibid.

Particular issues causing concern in the corridors of the Kremlin and eroding the trust between parties are basically NATO enlargement, which began in 1990s and its more recent decision of this decade to deploy missile defense systems in Poland and the Czech Republic. There are also other more general concerns of the Kremlin, such as the rise of Islamic terrorism and possible Arab Spring-like democratic movements in the Northern Caucasus and the Asia. In this sense, while Russia generally supports NATO and U.S. policies against terrorism, it finds their views and policies regarding the Arab Spring and social movements in the Middle East dangerous and against their national interests. It is concerned about the spread of these movements and increasing radicalization of marginal Islamist groups within and around its borders.

Moscow finds the current system unsuccessful in addressing the problems of the era and is in pursuit of a new security architecture for a new era, which nonetheless has some resonances of the old. Medvedev announced in 2008 Russia's desire for a new pan-European security system based on political and military integration of whole Euro-Atlantic area from Vancouver to Vladivostok. Two main reasons strengthen Russia's view on this. First, Russia has begun to see itself and its role in 21st century differently. After consolidation of economic and political power, it is confident of its regional geopolitical influence and also his potential to be a global one. This has changed Moscow's perception regarding Euro-Atlantic security design as well. Consequently, Moscow has been tailoring a more assertive and active role in Euro-Atlantic itself. Introduction of such a design would guarantee an equal say and equal status for Moscow. The second reason is the belief of Moscow that the current international system, its mechanisms and frameworks, is not working. Russia's proposal for new security architecture by asserting the deficiency of Euro-Atlantic security architecture, in this regard, is important. This initiative underscores Moscow's concerns about being left on the sidelines of decision-making mechanism of Euro-Atlantic security, arguments about its fragmentation, and confusion in the agendas of existing organizations. It is also a reaction to American unilateralism and seeks to create more multi-polar security system.[41]

C. NATO'S PERSPECTIVE

For all the structural problems and geopolitical challenges, because of its geographic space, economic potential, natural resources, nuclear capabilities, and foreign-policy influence, Russia is likely to remain a relevant regional and even global power in the foreseeable future.[42] Global economic crises and changing geopolitical balances that divert the U.S. strategic focus from Europe to Asia and the Pacific have significantly augmented the importance of Russia as a neighbor to both regions. Therefore, NATO Secretary General Anders Fogh Rasmussen, as of his first day in office, put NATO-Russia relations at the top of his agenda. However, the road has been rocky and bears many risks. Simply, there has not been a unity among NATO countries regarding how to deal with the Russia question. Karsten J. Moller asserts,

> The internal discussions on the New Strategic Concept [2010] are vivid proof of the profound disagreement. The 'old' members, e.g. Germany, France, Italy and now also the United States, wanted to expand cooperation with Russia in various fields while the new members, primarily Estonia, Latvia, Lithuania and Poland, supported by the Czech Republic and Hungary, looked with deep skepticism on cooperation with Russia, a skepticism founded in their historical experiences.[43]

From the first strategy document after the Cold War in 1991 to the latest, the 2010 strategic concept "active engagement, modern defense," Russia has remained a major theme in Allied calculations. However, post–Cold War strategic concepts have handled Russia with a different approach and nature. The 1991 strategic concept primarily focused on the end of the Cold War and concerns regarding NATO's raison d'être and

---

[41] Andrew Monaghan, introduction to *"Indivisibility of Security: Russia and Euro-Atlantic Security,"* ed. Andrew Monaghan, Forum Paper No.13, 5–25, NATO Defense College, January 2010.

[42] *"How Relevant is Russia to NATO As a Strategic Partner,"* Senior Course 117, Nato Defense College, January 2011.

[43] Karsten J. Moller, *"Russia and NATO after the Lisbon Summit: A New Beginning– Once Again?"* in Nato's New Strategic Concept: A Comprehensive Assessment, ed. Ringsmose and Sten Rynning, Danish Institute for International Studies Report 2011:02, 55–63.

purpose in the new era. According to it, Russia was no longer a strategic threat, but still a security challenge and a risk-bearing factor. In the following decade, such new threats as ethnic conflicts, economic distress, and the proliferation of WMD emerged and changed the strategic threat perceptions.

> The Washington Summit of 1999 . . . took place in the context of the Kosovo war and NATO's first round of enlargement into East Central Europe, and marked a high point of the Euro- Atlantic's ability to re-order the post communist East through the dual enlargement process (NATO and the EU) and humanitarian military intervention.[44]

On the other hand, the complexity of the challenges and the experiences in the Balkans reveal the need for dialogue and cooperation between NATO and Russia that extends beyond common rhetoric, and eventually this was reflected in the 1999 strategic concept in the form of an acknowledgement of Russia's unique position and its role in Euro-Atlantic security, and as a clear message to strengthen relations on the basis of common, interest, reciprocity and transparency within the framework of the Founding Act (1997).

At the NATO's anniversary summit in Strasbourg/Kehl in 2009, members agreed on the need for refining the strategic outlook of the Alliance and tasked the secretary general with drawing up a new strategic concept. A group of qualified experts, under the leadership of former U.S. secretary of state Madeleine Albright, developed recommendations for the NATO secretary general in a dialogue-oriented process. The group underwent its work in consultation with academics, journalists, decision makers, and international organizations in Moscow and Europe, and presented its report to Secretary General Rasmussen on 17 May 2010.[45] This report formed the basis of the new strategic concept adopted at Lisbon Summit in November 2010.

The 2010 strategic concept, "active engagement, modern defense," stresses the changing character of the security environment and the roles of Alliance. It is a product

---

[44] Adrian Hyde-Price, *"NATO's Political Transformation and International Order,"* in Nato's New Strategic Concept: A Comprehensive Assessment, *ed. Ringsmose and Sten Rynning, Danish Institute for International Studies Report 2011:02, 45–55.*

[45] Katsioulis, *"A Temporary Compromise."*

of an era shaped by the new security threats, crisis-management experiences in the Balkans and Afghanistan, and the benefits of cooperative partnerships.[46] Adrian Hyde claims,

> The Lisbon Summit and the New Strategic Concept, "Active Engagement, Modern Defense," were colored by two key international developments: the shifting global balance of power and the global recession. These two factors provide the key to understanding many of the political and strategic decisions reached in Lisbon, and are crucial in defining the structural context within which the Alliance now operates."[47]

It is important to deliberate the new strategic concept under the light of such facts as the power transition from a unipolar world to a multipolar one characterized by the rise of the BRIC countries (Brazil, Russia, India, and China) and global economic recession.

The 2010 concept summarizes, thus, the consensus reached in Lisbon by the member states; it inaugurates new approaches without laying down a fixed schedule, and positions NATO in the new security environment of the 21st century. It also describes NATO's core tasks and principles, values, and its strategic objectives for the next decade in an evolving security environment.[48] The content of the document centers around three core tasks: first, defense and deterrence that emphasizes the importance of Article 5 and the defensive alliance role, and second, crisis management that points out the necessity of taking action before, during, and after conflicts that pose risks to its security. Finally, promoting international security through cooperation requires the establishment of cooperative dialogues and partnerships with organization and states.[49]

In terms of NATO–Russia relations, the last task, cooperative security, deserves more attention. It is rather related to the political aspect of the Alliance. NATO, within this context, concentrates its political efforts in three areas: first, arms control,

---

[46] *Strategic Concepts*, NATO Official Webpage, http://www nato.int/cps/en/natolive/topics_56626.htm

[47] Hyde-Price, *"NATO's Political Transformation."*

[48] Katsioulis, *"A Temporary Compromise."*

[49] Klauss Wittmann, *"An Alliance for the 21st Century? Reviewing NATO's New Strategic Concept,"* in Nato's New Strategic Concept: A Comprehensive Assessment, *ed. Ringsmose and Sten Rynning, Danish Institute for International Studies Report 2011:02, 31–43.*

disarmament, and non-proliferation; second, enlargement; and third, partnerships. NATO stresses on the need for improvement in relations with Russia and states that its intent is to develop a "real strategic partnership" based on common interests and challenges. To this end, the strategic concept suggests greater transparency in terms of arsenals and reciprocal disarmament, greater focus for conventional arms-control regimes, and broader consultation with Russia. Thence, it emphasizes the importance of the NATO-Russia Council and indexes full utilization of it.[50] Furthermore, unlike the previous one, it does not mention imminent joining of new member states, notwithstanding underscoring its open-door policy to all European democracies. Particularly, it does not refer to Georgia and Ukraine by name, observing Russia's sensitivity.[51]

In practical terms, Adrian Hyde suggests,

The Lisbon Summit was the occasion for resetting the Russia–NATO relationship, based on three tangible areas of cooperation: first, revamping the NATO–Russia Council, which has long been regarded as an ineffective talking-shop . . . Second, cooperation on theatre missile defense: a NATO–Russia Council working group on missile defense will be resumed, focusing on creating an 'Active Layered Theatre Ballistic Missile Defense' (ALTBMD). Third, cooperation on Afghanistan: Russia will aid NATO by keeping open land supply routes for non-lethal materials and will provide assistance with helicopters to the Afghan security forces.[52]

In a nutshell, "One of the primary achievements of the Lisbon Summit and a key manifestation of the changing constellation of global power relations was the forging of a new, more cooperative relationship with the Russian Federation."[53] The final draft of the strategic concept interprets the desire of the NATO countries to improve constructive relations with Russia and move towards a full-fledged strategic partnership.[54] It has become quite obvious that incongruity in the NATO–Russia relations casts a shadow on peace and stability in Europe and puts a strain on all Euro-Atlantic security. It is

[50] Katsioulis, *"A Temporary Compromise."*

[51] Ibid.

[52] Hyde-Price, *"NATO's Political Transformation."*

[53] Ibid.

[54] Monaghan, *"From Lisbon to Munich."*

particularly important to note that NATO and Russia agree on ongoing differences between each other and openly acknowledge their (well known) disagreements in the overcast atmosphere after the Georgian War, and desire to move forward and get over them. Thereby, as Klaus Wittmann argues, "The Lisbon Summit [can be] interpreted as a breakthrough in NATO's cooperation with Russia and as a contribution "to creating a common space of peace, stability and security."[55]

To conclude, NATO's perspective regarding Russia embraces a non-confrontational relationship, which would hopefully transformed in to a "true strategic partnership," on the basis of mutual trust and transparency that is essential for peace and stability in the Euro-Atlantic region. Mindful of their differences and problems and willing to eliminate them over the course of time, NATO sees Russia as a potential strategic partner that continuously needs to be monitored. All past strategic concepts, summit declarations, statements of leaders and top-level officials underline the significance of improving relations with Russia. Russia has been and continues to be a relevant actor in Euro-Atlantic security, whom NATO has to and does seek to engage.

---

[55] *Wittmann, "An Alliance for the 21st Century?"*

THIS PAGE INTENTIONALLY LEFT BLANK

III. GEOPOLITICS OF RUSSIA, DISTINCT RUSSIAN IDENTITY, AND THEIR IMPLICATIONS ON FOREIGN-POLICY DECISIONS OF MOSCOW

Moscow's foreign-policy making is shaped and influenced by many factors that also determine the prospects of a sound partnership with NATO, more broadly with the West. The perspectives of the West and Russia in conceptualizing international order and making their foreign policy decisions diverge in many respects. Above all others, the geopolitics of Russia and Russian people's perceived identity are primary factors shaping the relations of Russia with the West, and cause divergence. This chapter will analyze, first, how the geopolitics and geography of Russia influence Russian foreign policy decisions and lead to friction in Russia–NATO relations. Second it will explore how Russian identity and its components, European and Asian cultures, historical setting, and Orthodox Christianity render Russo-Western relations problematic.

A. GEOGRAPHY AND GEOPOLITICS

Russia's geography and geopolitics provide an inhospitable home for its peoples. Even though the country is full of natural resources, a harsh climate and scarcity of the arable lands in addition to strategic disadvantages have led the Russian people to experience a history more full of violent and sorrowful days than glorious and happy ones. The invasions of Nordic peoples, Western armies (Napoleon and Hitler), and Eastern Nomadic nations (Tatars, Mongols, and Turks) and the oppression of their own rulers have led them to experience tough lives in a harsh geography. Distilled from past experience and current geopolitical realities, Russian conceptualizations of the global order and international relations can be defined in rather realistic and rationalist terms.

As throughout history, geography and the geopolitical position of Russia are two key determinant factors in understanding Russian foreign -policy behavior in the 21st century. They have provided both obstacles and opportunities for Russian–Western relations by influencing Russian foreign policy behavior both directly and indirectly. Their direct impact is related to its territorial features and its geographic position, which determines its neighbors and the regional political environment. On the other hand, indirectly, their impact on Russia's security, defense, economy, and culture indirectly contribute to the forming of Moscow's foreign-policy behavior. In addition, the perceptions and understanding of the elites, important factors in the making of foreign policy, predominantly rely on geopolitical and geographical conditions. Hence, Robert Donaldson and Joseph Nogee suggest "The foreign policy of Russia—whether in its tsarist, its Soviet, or its democratic form—is an expression in some measure of certain relatively fixed geopolitical realities."[56]

Geography and geopolitical position are two important factors in designing the security and defense of a country. In this sense, George Friedman claims "Russia's defining characteristic is its indefensibility."[57] Russia's core geography in particular, where the medieval Grand Principality of Muscovy was located, is devoid of natural defensive features. It lacks rivers, seas, or mountain ranges on which to rely for defense. Russia has always tended to compensate for this vulnerability by expanding whenever possible. As a response to continual invasions from west and east, it embraced a strategy of expansion and establishing buffers, which came to be characterized as the main foreign policy behavior of Russia over time. Thus, Russians developed an obsession with security caused by geopolitical and geographic realities—vulnerability to invasions, difficulty of maintaining internal order—which can be argued to constitute the main motivation behind the expansionist behavior of Russia.[58] "At one level," Thomas Graham points out, "Moscow's fear is a product of Russia's geopolitical setting, political structure and historical experience, all of which have shaped its strategic culture."[59] Even today, this insecurity, ossified into Russian strategic thinking, constitutes one of the main impediments for closer partnership between Russia and the West. John Erickson suggests that a combination of despair and defiance in the 1990s, caused by the huge crisis of identity and a challenge to its security with the collapse of Soviet Union, is the reason for

---

[56] Robert H. Donaldson and Joseph L. Nogee, *The Foreign Policy of Russia: Changing Systems, Enduring Interests* (NY: M.E. Sharpe, April 18, 2009), 16.

[57] George Friedman, *The Geopolitics of Russia: Permanent Struggle, Stratfor,* October 15, 2008 http://www.stratfor.com/sample/analysis/geopolitics-russia-permanent-struggle.

[58] Donaldson and Nogee, *Changing Systems, Enduring Interest,* 29.

[59] Thomas Graham, *"The Sources of Russia's Insecurity,"* Survival: Global Politics and Strategy, 52:1 (2010): 56. http://dx.doi.org/10.1080/00396331003612471

the current obsessive preoccupation of Russians with geopolitics and global power configurations and their relevance to key issues of Russian national security.[60] As a result, Russian policymakers have come to believe in the supremacy of realpolitik in international relations and conceptualize the international system according to its imperatives. They assume that every nation seeks to increase its security and enlarge its sphere of influence, and it needs to enhance its hard and soft power to be able to do so. Therefore, Russian strategic thinking places a priority on military capabilities over political ones.[61]

It is impossible to ignore the existence of the sense of insecurity, solidly entrenched into Russian strategic thinking over the centuries, especially in the foreign-policy thinking of the elites and policymakers of the 21st century. This deep-seated angst finds venues of expression in Eurasianists and Centrist ideologies, the strongest supporters of which are military elites and members of security and intelligence services known as the *siloviki*. For instance, Mankoff asserts that, more than economic growth and other factors, Sir Halford John Mackinder's precepts about "controlling the heartland" still preoccupy the minds of elites and policymakers in Moscow.[62] Thus, it is fair to assert that the sense of insecurity, a natural outcome of Russia's geography and geopolitical imperatives, influences foreign-policy behavior in the 21st century by settling into the mindsets of the elites who are the main actors in the making of the Russian Federation's foreign policy.

Since Ivan III, Russian rulers' basic principle of Russian foreign policy and strategy has mostly been the survival of the state, and then to find ways to promote its security by expanding or winning time to regenerate.[63] In accordance with this principle, Moscow, aware of the weakness of its economic and defense capabilities today, seeks

---

[60] John Erickson, "*Russia Will Not Be Trifled with: Geopolitical Facts and Fantasies,*" Journal of Strategic Studies, Volume 22, Issue 2–3, 1999, 243. DOI: 10.1080/01402399908437763

[61] Trenin, "*Russia's Threat Perception and Strategic Posture.*"

[62] Jeffrey Mankoff, *Russian Foreign Policy: The Return of Great Power Politics*, (NY: Rowman & Littlefield Publishers Inc., 2009), 73.

[63] Donaldson and Nogee, *Changing Systems, Enduring Interest*, 66.

global stability while focusing on domestic consolidation.[64] Erickson asserts that Russia as a state first "aims at attaining ease within itself," and second at establishing an independent "great space" around itself. He also claims in this regard that Russia appreciates "the primacy of economic well-being and social stability as the guarantor of national security."[65] Accordingly, Thomas Graham states in his article, *'The Sources of Russia's Insecurity'* that

> at all times the survival of the empire and the maintenance of its territorial integrity were the paramount priorities for Russia's rulers, before which national, religious, economic and other priorities invariably yielded.[66]

Consequently, it could be argued that Russian rulers have always had to balance the dual task of defending or advancing borders and maintaining domestic order.[67] The challenge for Moscow since the break-up of the USSR, in this regard, has been regenerating the Russian economy, enhancing the domestic social order, and winning time while trying to preserve regional and global geopolitical influence

This dual task of ensuring internal and external security has necessitated strong and effective security and intelligence services in addition to a powerful standing military. This has led to the consolidation of military and bureaucratic power within the Russian state. This reality existed both in the tsarist and Soviet eras. Even today, the military and the bureaucracy continue to play strong roles in domestic politics and in the making of foreign policy, though at a reduced level. On the other hand, Russian rulers' and policymakers' second concern, ensuring social cohesion and maintenance of order at home, has been a natural consequence of an over-extended territory consisting of a multi-ethnic and multi-religious society and politically unstable buffers. Holding the vast empire together in the face of centrifugal forces has led to the centralization of political authority and power and has given way to highly centralized governments throughout Russian history, the latest of which is the Putin administration. Authoritarian government

---

[64] Mankoff, *The Return of Great Power Politics*, 39.

[65] Erickson, *Russia Will Not Be Trifled*, 257.

[66] Graham, *The Sources of Russia's Insecurity*, 55.

[67] Ibid., 57.

and the tendency towards centralization in economics and governance can, in this respect, be considered a consequence of Russian geography and geopolitics.

Russia's loss of buffer spaces with the disintegration of the USSR and its lack of defensible borders in its current situation has constituted a huge crisis for Russian strategic thinking, given the history of invasions, internal disorders, and deep-seated insecurity. John Erickson expresses similar thoughts by presenting more concrete evidence in conformity with the 21st century's geostrategic thinking:

> A shrunken Russia lost heavily in the geostrategic and geo-economic stakes: reduced access to the sea, loss of port facilities, shut off as a 'northern-continental country' like some obscure corner of Europe. Russia was deprived of key elements of its strategic early warning system and air defense capabilities, vulnerability magnified by the reduction in the number of airfields available. The security of lengthy land and maritime frontiers fell to a shrinking military force.[68]

Consequently, the overemphasis in Russian foreign policy agendas on relations with the members of the Commonwealth of Independent States (CIS)—for instance, in the so-called Medvedev Doctrine of 2008 and recently in Putin's executive order on foreign policy in 2012—can be considered part of the outcome of Russia's traditional reflex of expanding and establishing buffers in a bid for security, although via more peaceful methods this time. In this regard, Russian overreaction and opposition to NATO enlargement, which has already penetrated into the area of "privileged interests" and happens to include some CIS members, is quite understandable.

Russia's geography and geopolitical position have negative consequences for its economy and foreign policy, even though it possesses rich natural resources. In addition to the vastness of its territory, unfavorable weather conditions render any commercial activity impossible in some regions, hinder exploitation of some resources, cripple transportation, and complicate the establishment of a sustainable trade network within the country. Its geopolitical position also denies direct access to oceanic ports and global trade routes and circumvents foreign trade. The absence of ice-free ports, needed on commercial and military grounds, concerns Moscow much and constitutes another

---

[68] Erickson, *Russia Will Not Be Trifled*, 246.

motivation for Russia's expansionist behavior.[69] Moreover, the shortage of arable lands limits the production of foods and sometimes leads the Russian state to fail in meeting the demands of population. Thus, Russian geography hinders the creation of a strong diversified economy, leads to foreign trade dominated by the exportation of natural resources, creates vulnerability, and prevents Russia from pursuing more assertive foreign policies.

In the 21st century, despite the economic and political achievements of the Putin administration, a fundamental threat to Russia's territorial and political integrity continues to exist. However, it is different from former threats. The global economic and geopolitical order is starkly different from twenty years before. Unlike before, other dynamic political entities and regions are active in Russia's traditional sphere of influence. China and India keep rising politically and economically in the East and South. Russia is also quite concerned about the threat of fundamentalist Islam to Central Asia, emanating from Afghanistan and Pakistan in the South. And last but not least, Europe lies to the West and remains an influential actor in global economics and politics in spite of the current crisis. Contrary to the former Russia's dynamism and outward expansionist pattern, today there is contraction in the geopolitical space of Russia and dynamism in the regions surrounding it.[70]

Russo–Sino relations need more elaboration. China is the most imminent potential threat for Moscow, particularly given Russia's demographic decline, especially in its Far East, despite seemingly good relations between the two political entities. Like other global powers, China's rise means a lot to Russia. Its proximity to Russian borders and strategic backyard—Central Asia—causes concern and fear, even if the Kremlin does not let it show. China's growing interest, political and economic influence, and energy investments in Central Asia, for instance, which Russia considers its backyard, undermine Russia's interests and deprive it of the political leverage it has been using

---

[69] Donaldson and Nogee, *Changing Systems, Enduring Interest,* 29.

[70] Graham, *The Sources of Russia's Insecurity,* 62–3.

against Central Asian countries.[71] Long-standing territorial issues in the Far East—notwithstanding they were resolved during Putin's first term as president—and the growing demographic, economic, and political influence of China, both within the eastern borders of Russia and former Soviet space, ignite concerns in the corridors of the Kremlin, no matter how much Putin administration tries to hold it back and establish better relations with China. Realistically, Moscow has no other option. To Lo, it is the only way for Russia to reconcile a resurgent China and create a protective mechanism against this power rising along its eastern borders.[72] Kaczmarski asserts that Russians are aware of the shift of balance in favor of China and the waning of U.S. hegemony that "served as glue" for Russian-Chinese cooperation; however, they lack the capacity to end this engagement.[73] On the other hand, according to Kuchins, Russia's close engagement with China has been considered a part of its counterbalancing behavior against Western dominance.[74] In sum, strategic convenience, pragmatism and a commonality of interests serve as the basis for the Russia-China partnership in today's geopolitical setting.[75]

In the 2000s, the shift of power in the strategic equation in Southeast Asia has become more apparent and the economic and demographic gap between Russia and China has become even larger; ergo, Russia will be paying more attention to resurgent China rising along its eastern border and deliberating more on Asian geopolitics. Russia will have to stop hiding its concern and overtly face the reality and seek to counterbalance China by either building closer ties with the West or finding allies in South and East Asia. In this sense, some scholars regard the reset in U.S.-Russia relations, as evidence of Russia's covert concern over rising China. Russia, overall,

---

[71] Marcin Kaczmarski, *Domestic Sources of Russia's China Policy*, Problems of Post - Communism, 59(2), (Mar/Apr 2012): 3, 6, Accessed June 25, 2012.
http://search.proquest.com/docview/1013444519?accountid=12702.

[72] Bobo Lo, Axis of convenience : Moscow, Beijing, and the New Geopolitics, (London, Washington, DC: Brookings Institution Press: 2008), 44, cited in Marcin Kaczmarski, *Domestic Sources of Russia's China Policy*, Problems of Post - Communism, 59(2), (Mar/Apr 2012): 3, 3,
http://search.proquest.com/docview/1013444519?accountid=12702.

[73] Andrew Kuchins, "Russian Perspectives on China: Strategic Ambivalence," In The Future of China-Russia Relations, ed. Bellacqua, cited in Kaczmarski, *Domestic Sources of Russia's China Policy*, 4.

[74] Kaczmarski, *Domestic Sources of Russia's China Policy*, 5.

[75] Ibid., 4.

seems to be securing itself by seeking a balance between aligning with other powers and engaging China politically and economically. Considering the U.S.'s concerns over Southeast Asian and its shift of focus toward this region, along with China's rise, will serve as an incentive for increased cooperation between the U.S. and Russia, and accordingly between NATO and Russia.[76]

Russian identity is also to some extent a function of geography and geopolitical position. Extending from Europe to the Bering Sea, Russia possesses an identity combining European and Asian cultural elements. Whether Russia is Asian or European has been widely debated among elites and politicians, both in the West and Russia, for centuries. The answer of the Russian people to the question of who they are is important, since the perceived identity of a country matters much in establishing foreign-policy goals. Commenting on the foreign-policy goals of 21st century Russia, Mankoff asserts, "The new approach to foreign policy rested on a deep-seated consensus among the Russian elite about the nature of international relations and about the identity of Russia as a state."[77] Therefore, it is meaningful to analyze Russian identity and culture with respect to their influence on Russian foreign policy and, accordingly, on Russia's relations with the West.

B. RUSSIAN IDENTITY

Russian identity, a product of a consensus among Russian public opinion and elites, is the other key determinant factor providing foundations for Russian foreign policy and influencing Russian–NATO relations. Identity influences Russia's foreign policy decisions, most importantly by shaping the perceptions of the Russian elites and common people. The subject of furious debate during the past twenty years, Russian identity, accordingly, is an essential element in Russian strategic thinking and provides both opportunities and obstacles in the troubled relations between Russia and the West.

---

[76] Ibid., 4–7.

[77] Mankoff, *The Return of Great Power Politics*, 11.

Identity is a highly complex concept, comprising the elements of history, culture, social psychology, and politics.[78] In the Russian case, also, the people's knotty history, the legacy of two hundred years of Mongol–Turkic Horde rule (between 1238 and 1480), hundreds of years of tsarist rule that gave Russians both suffering and pride, the impact of Prince Vladimir's choice of Orthodox Christianity, the experience with socialism, the social policies of Stalin, geography, geopolitics, and finally the breakup of a great political project combined in the formation of Russian identity. And of course, contemporary developments keep molding it every moment, since identity is a dynamic, not a stagnant, concept and keeps evolving over time. Russian identity, as well, keeps being influenced by global developments, international interactions, and domestic experiences, evolving dynamically over the course of time. That is to say, contemporary political and economic currents within and outside of the borders of Russia and the relations with foreign entities are influencing, and being influenced by, Russian identity.

It is beneficial here to look at what the contemporary agreed-upon Russian identity is and how it has taken shape after the disappearance of the political ideology and dissolution of the USSR. We will then analyze the ideological streams and debates on what it means to be a Russian.

Russia has an identity divided between West and the East, autocratic past and democratic aspirations, and realities of the day and nostalgia for a "glorious" past. Throughout history, Russian rulers and thinkers tried to answer whether Russia is culturally and socially closer to the West or the East, and whether it belongs to Eastern or Western civilization, or both, or neither. What it means to be a Russian is relevant in conceptualizing the nature of its international politics and formation of foreign-policy perceptions and behaviors, since culture affects the strategic behavior of a country.

It is almost impossible to define "the Russians" anatomically, physiologically, or genetically since the biological heritage of the Russians is extremely diverse. Russians are widely considered to descend from such different ethnic groups as Finns, Ukrainians, Tatars, Mongols, Germans, Swedes, etc. Even in the core of Russia, the region around

---

[78] Peter J S. Duncan, *"Contemporary Russian Identity between East and West."* The Historical Journal 48. 1 (March 2005): 282.

Moscow, the Russians are not from a single ancestral group.[79] "Russianness" has been a term constructed psychologically, socially, or culturally, but certainly not biologically. This is not to say that a sense of nationhood grew in Russian lands. A national consciousness, a national identity, or a nation-state building process did not develop throughout Russian history.

Both in the imperial and Soviet era, formation of a nation and a nation state was ignored; Russians failed to develop an ethnic consciousness and solidarity. However, the Soviet system contributed to the emergence of a national consciousness. The use of Russian as a lingua franca, the Russian-dominated leadership, and the national victory against Nazi Germany nurtured this identity to a certain extent.[80] In addition, Donaldson and Nogee point out:

> Russia has never existed as a nation-state; rather, during both the tsarist and Soviet periods it had been multinational empire with messianic ambitions. Unlike other European imperial states, the modern Russian nation was not formed prior to the period of colonial expansion. Moreover, the tsars, unlike the rulers of Britain or France, colonized lands that bordered on their home territories, thus producing an unusual intermixing of Russian and non-Russian peoples.[81]

Dmitri Trenin notes accordingly, "Post-imperial Russia did not experience a rebirth as a nation-state, like post–World War II democratic Germany or the republican Kemalist Turkey. It did not shrink to a small fragment, a souvenir of past imperial glory, like post-1918 Deutsch-Oesterreich, which became the Republic of Austria."[82] Consequently, during the imperial experiences in the tsarist and Soviet eras, Russia failed to develop a strong sense of nationhood; above all, the multinational character of tsarist and Soviet Russia curbed the development of such a sense, as Peter Duncan asserts. He goes on to explain that the dissolution of the Soviet state and ideology's official power left a "conceptual void" in foreign-policy thinking and national identity. Hence, Yeltsin,

---

[79] Daniel Rancour-Laferriere, *Russian Nationalism From an Interdisciplinary Perspective: Imagining Russia* (New York: The Edwin Mellen Press, 2000), 89.

[80] Duncan, *Contemporary Russian Identity between East and West*, 283.

[81] Donaldson and Nogee, *Changing Systems, Enduring Interest,* 110.

[82] Dmitri Trenin, *Post-Imperium: a Eurasian story*, (Washington, DC: Carnegie Endowment for International Peace, 2011), 37.

later found it sensible to create a civic identity, which maintains a multiethnic and multi-religious character that provides a legitimate basis for the post-Soviet Russian Federation.[83]

Since the beginning of 1990s, with the break-up of the USSR—and even a little before, Russia has been experiencing an identity crisis. "Stripped of the geopolitical and ideological certainties at the heart of Soviet politics, contemporary Russia has been forced to answer a series of fundamental questions about its relationship to the post–Cold War world system and its own identity as a state," Jeffrey Mankoff suggests.[84] Gorbachev and Yeltsin's answer to this crisis was Westernization, embracing the democratic and free-market values of the West, getting rid of all the legacies of the totalitarian past, and constructing a new civic identity that would encompass all ethnic groups within its vast borders. Defining citizens in purely civic terms was certainly a brave attempt that would bring all peoples within the borders of Russia under a common roof, given that the communist or nationalist opposition has not welcomed promotion of such a civic identity.[85] With respect to the deep question of a definition for Russian identity, Vera Tolz provides five different perspectives prevalent in the post-Soviet period:

1. The Union, or imperial, identity sees the Russians as destined to create and maintain a multi-national state. This includes nationally minded communists, ultra-nationalists and Eurasianists. Russia, in whatever form, must be great power and a strong state.

2. The view that assumes the Russian nation as a community of Eastern Slavs comprised of Russians, Ukrainians, and, Belarusians. Those branches of "East Slavonic tree" speak close languages; share a common faith, Orthodox Christianity. Alexander Solzhenitsyn is the most prominent adherent of this view that suggests a federation among three states or of their union in a single all-Russian state.

3. Russian nation is comprised of the people who use Russian as their first language whatever their ethnicity is. That requires redrawing of Russian frontiers and lacks a significant political support.

---

[83] Duncan, *Contemporary Russian Identity between East and West*, 277.

[84] Mankoff, *The Return of Great Power Politics*, 11.

[85] Dale G. Torgersen, "Kto I Kuda? *Russia, Language, and National Identity*" (Master's Thesis, Naval Postgraduate School, 2009).

4. A racial definition of Russianness by blood that aims excluding Jews and peoples from the Caucasus and Central Asia.

5. A civic definition that embraces all citizens of the Russian Federation.[86]

Among them, the civic definition has been officially accepted in the post-Soviet Era. On November 28, 1991, the law adopted by the Russian Federation refers to Russian citizens in strictly civic terms, i.e., *Rossiiane*.[87] And later, Yeltsin and then Putin adopted the promotion of a civic identity and a non-ethnic definition of nationhood, and have also used the word *Rossiianin*, which does not have an ethnic connotation, instead of *Russkii*. However, leaders in practice have tended to extend the definition of ethnic Russianness to include the Russian-speaking population, in some part because of the demands and necessities of the new demographic distribution in Russia. It has never been an easy task to take into account the proportion of the ethnic Russian-speaking population in the Russian Federation, which, unlike in the Soviet era, during when they composed slightly more than half the population, now account for four-fifths of the population, while such ethnic minorities as Chechens and Tatars now form a tenth. On the other hand, growing support for nationalists and communists has rendered the extension in the definition of identity inevitable. That is to say, currently accepted civic identity in Russia, in some ways, reconciles the demands of the people and goals of policymakers and elites and transcends the civic definition tilting toward ethnicity.[88]

The rising support for communism and the nostalgia for the great Soviet past led President Boris Yeltsin to relax the civic definition of the Russian identity and temper the stance of categorical rejection of the communist legacy. As a result of the continuing presence of the imperial and Soviet legacies, Yeltsin even had to bring back the imperial two-headed eagle as the state emblem. Putin later took over this stance of Yeltsin's and went even further, praising the achievements of the Soviet Union in many of his public speeches. Putin, restored the Soviet national anthem as the Russian Federation's anthem,

---

[86] Vera Tolz, *Russia: Inventing the Nation*, (London and New York: Oxford University Press, 2001), 235–60 cited in Peter J S. Duncan, "*Contemporary Russian Identity between East and West*." The Historical Journal 48:1 (Mar 2005): 285.

[87] Vera Tolz, "Politicians' Conceptions of the Russian Nation," in *Contemporary Russian Politics: A Reader*, ed. Archie Brown (New York: Oxford University Press, 2001), 355.

[88] Duncan, Contemporary Russian Identity between East and West, 283–86.

with a few alterations in lyrics. Both Yeltsin and his successor, Putin, sought to reconcile the new civic identity of the Russian Federation with the positive aspects of tsarist and Soviet legacies that could be useful for promoting a multiethnic identity.[89]

C.   ANTI-WESTERN SENTIMENT?

Russian nationalism has gained strength in the post-Soviet era as a reaction to unfavorable conditions and political developments as well as enduring features of political culture and tradition. In addition to nostalgia for the past, poor economic conditions, over-subordination to the West, and enlargement of NATO into Eastern Europe have nurtured nationalist feelings in the Russian elite and people. Reaction to these factors and the deep-seated insecurities of Russians came together, and a wave of anti-Westernism took root in Russian politics.[90]

Putin's nationalism is essentially state-centered, and pragmatic in many ways.[91] It is neither obsessively nationalist nor anti-Western; it is, rather, pragmatic. According to Duncan, in a comparison that may apply to the 21st century or not, "The regime [Putin's era] was reminiscent of Peter the Great, who introduced some Westernizing reforms while strengthening autocracy and serfdom."[92] While consolidating centralized power and pursuing economic reform at home, Putin has sought to cooperate with the West to obtain trade and technology, in order to strengthen the state, as Peter did in the beginning of the eighteenth century with the European system and the society of his age at which time such reform from above was the norm in the northern courts of the Romanovs, the Hohenzollerns and the Habsburgs. The leadership rejects ethnic Russian nationalism, seeing itself as the heir of the Soviet multinational state. It forcibly incorporated the Chechens and is still putting economic and political pressure on some of the former

---

[89] Ibid., 286–7.

[90] Ibid., 287.

[91] Ibid., 294.

[92] Duncan, Contemporary Russian Identity between East and West, 283–86

Soviet republics. The use of both tsarist and Soviet symbols reflect that the Russian Federation was far from being a nation-state, but neither did it attempt to revive the empire.

Russia has always been confused between nostalgia for the past and the attraction towards the West. The conflict between these two incompatible ideas has never been resolved throughout modern Russian history. Russia's troubled journey toward the West started with the energetic and enthusiastic ruler Peter the Great in the seventeenth century. Stunned by the developments and progress of the West, Peter had always aspired for the Russian Empire to achieve the West's level of civilization. He believed that by following the Western way and adopting Western institutions without question, Russia could bridge the gap with the West. His reforms and efforts left an indelible impact on the Russian psyche. The West has always set the standard for Russia to reach or overtake. On the other hand, beginning from Peter's era, opposition to the idea of Westernization has never ceased. The Slavophiles suggested promoting Russian tradition and Russian culture rather than simply copying the West. For the Slavophiles, Russian tradition and culture meant what they imagined to be Russian society before Peter the Great. Struggles between Slavophiles and Westernizers have been an intrinsic part of Russian politics.[93]

The essential difference between Slavophiles and Westernizers was over the question of whether, in borrowing from European culture, Russia was rejecting its own nature and culture or taking the necessary steps for its regeneration and progress: Slavophiles supported the former, Westernizers the latter.[94] The struggle between them gained new strength with the collapse of the Soviet Union. Amid the social, economic, and moral ruins of the empire, between nostalgia for the past and the promise of the West, Russian people were to decide their own fate. Duncan summarizes the situation as follows:

> The centuries-old question regarding whether Russia should become part of the West, or follow its own unique Eastern path, acquired new interest

---

[93] Torgersen, *Russia, Language, and National Identity*.

[94] Geoffrey Hosking, *Russia and the Russians: A History* (Cambridge: The Belknap Press of Harvard University Press, 2001), 277.

after the collapse of the Soviet Union in December 1991. For Westernizers in Russia, the 'West' symbolized progress, freedom, democracy, civil society, normality, and a nation-state. Their opponents saw the West as representing capitalist exploitation, moral decadence, and American dominance. Westernizers saw the 'East' as linked with autocracy, despotism, and empire. Their opponents admired precisely these features, which for them signified a strong state, unity, and order.[95]

Richard Sakwa suggests, "As in all countries, but particularly in those which once gloried in an imperial past, the present is viewed through the prism of historical concerns and achievements. In the Russian case this is reinforced by a double historical tradition, the Soviet and the tsarist."[96] The past imperial power achieved by first tsarist and then Soviet Russia is always a temptation and motivation for following a distinct track from the West's, no matter how strong the promise of the West. Sakwa also claims that this "self-appreciation" of Russia, caused partly by its imperial experiences, is the reason behind the Russia's problematic relationship with the hegemonic international system. Moscow's demand to maintain its autonomy and to be treated on equal terms arguably caused by the same reason, according to Sakwa. Overall, one of the unique features of the post-Soviet Russian reassertion has been the intersection of great-power status and democratic agendas, which clearly reflect the dilemma of the Russian psyche.[97]

Russia's second dilemma has been its indecisiveness regarding democracy and autocracy. While Western values gradually took hold in Russian culture, beginning with Peter I, Russia's distinct religious track (since 988), the strong influence of Mongol, Tatar, and Turkic heritages, and experience with communism have driven a wider wedge with the West. Russia's Asiatic features inherited from the Mongols and their successor Turkic Khanates remain influential in the culture, society, and state. Richard Pipes asserts that Moscow learned about kingship and central authority "as a working institution" from the Golden Horde; and Russian historians attribute a significant role to Mongols in the

---

[95] Duncan, *Contemporary Russian Identity between East and West*, 277.

[96] Richard Sakwa, "Russia's Identity: Between the 'Domestic' and the 'International'," Europe-Asia Studies, 63:6,(2011), 957–975 http://dx.doi.org/10.1080/09668136.2011.585749

[97] Ibid., 957.

formation of Russian statehood.[98] Under the absolute domination of the Golden Horde, Muscovy inherited all the state institutions of the "*Sarai*," the capital of the Golden Horde, most importantly the central political authority. The large volume of Turkic and Tatar vocabulary in state terminology, such as treasury *kazna* and turnover tax *tamga*, is evidence of this influence. On the other hand, Russia inherited many institutions and ecclesiastical traditions, including the title "tsar" for their emperors, from Byzantine, which put distance between Russia and the Western Roman Empire, and thus the West, since the sixth century. Overall, it is sensible to argue that Mongol, Turkic, and Byzantine influence on Russian culture impede its integration with the West.[99]

Patrimonialism and statism, in this regard, are important aspects of Russian identity that reflect its eastern ancestry and heritage. Russians, both in the tsarist and Soviet eras, chose to subordinate individual interests for group interests or state interest—a custom not unknown to continental Europeans in turn. The primacy of the group has always been in the Russian psyche. Taking into account the Turkic and Mongol patrimonial and collectivist thinking, favoring group needs over individual needs, that distilled into Russian culture, it could be argued that Russia lacks individualism, a defining characteristic of the West, as a result of its interactions with the Asian societies.

The experience with communism had also great impact on Russian culture. It aggravated the centuries old political cultural cleavages between the Orthodox world and Western Christianity, namely between Russia and the West. Building upon the Golden Horde legacy, communism consolidated authoritarianism in Russia. After all, in the wake of the collapse of communism, it would be very naïve to expect Russian society to adopt Westernization and democratic values overnight, inasmuch as change in a culture requires a certain time span.[100]

Ronald Inglehart argues that culture is "past dependent," and if the effects of economic development are controlled, different societies, such as historically Protestant,

---

[98] Richard Pipes, *Russia Under the Old Regime*, (London: Weidenfeld and Nicolson, 1974), 74.

[99] Ibid., 72–5.

[100] Ronald Inglehart, "Culture and Democracy," in Lawrence E. Harrison and Samuel P. Huntington, eds., *Culture Matters* (New York: Basic Books, 2000), 86.

Orthodox, Islamic, or Confucian societies, develop highly distinctive value systems.[101] He categorizes societies in two ways: first in terms of survival versus secular rational orientations. To him, while societies that have survival values and traditional orientation have autocratic tendencies, societies that emphasize self-expression are much more likely to be stable democracies.[102] According to the global cultural map, prepared from data collected between 1995 and 1998 by the World Values Survey, Russia belongs in the orthodox group with other ex-Communist countries, possessing survival values with an emphasis on economic and physical security.[103]

> A society's position on the survival/self-expression index is strongly correlated with its level of democracy, as indicated by its scores on the Freedom House ratings of political rights and civil liberties from 1972 through 1998. This relationship is powerful. Virtually all of the societies that rank high on survival/self-expression values are stable democracies; virtually all that rank low has authoritarian governments.[104]

It can be concluded from the graphic also, that democracy flourishes in some social and cultural contexts more than in others, and in this regard the cultural conditions of Russia and other ex-democratic countries in the 1990s was not favorable for democracy. Therefore, it would not be sensible to expect a sudden change in Russia and that liberal democratic values flourish there overnight.

History, culture, religion, ideology, and geography all, hand-in-hand, consolidated the autarky and oppression within the borders of the Russia. All new ideas or reform movements unexceptionally developed from top to bottom and were applied through violence and coercion until the end of the 20th century. From Peter's Westernization campaign to Stalin's industrialization efforts, this reality has not changed. In the late 20th century, with the help of leaders such as Gorbachev and Yeltsin, and the media and press, which enable ideas to spread into every layer of society, the Russian people had a chance to break this continuity. However, the realities of Russia have impeded, or at least,

---

[101] Ibid., 82.

[102] Ibid., 84.

[103] Ibid., 85.

[104] Ibid., 94.

slowed down the Westernization stream, and Russia's dilemma between democracy and autarky keeps prevailing in domestic political life.

According to James Billington, "The central struggle in the Soviet break with its totalitarian past has been between physical power and moral authority, between a dictatorial machine trying to control things at the top and a movement toward democracy from below."[105] He argues that the awakening Russian people will be the main actor in determining the result of the conflict between deap-seated authoritarianism and bottom-up democracy movement.[106] Looking at developments in last two decades, the former has gained strength, whereas the latter has worn off. However, considering the presence of popular support and demand for democracy, the chance of Putin's ignoring it and taking a big political risk in the future is quite low.

D.   CONTESTING IDEOLOGIES

How a state defines itself as statecraft and political culture is a key factor influencing its foreign policy, with respect to how it conceptualizes international politics and its position in the international stage in constructivist terms. Its area of interest and influence, in what alliances it should participate in, and many other questions regarding its strategic interests and decisions are quite relevant to its definition of itself. Naturally, an agreed-upon identity is shaped by many factors, ranging from culture and history to geography. And it is usually a product of a rocky process of conflicting views or ideologies ending with a compromise or domination of one over others. Conflicting views are influenced by each other; there is give and take. In the Russian case as well, the 21st century agreed-upon identity is the product of a long process, synthesizing many views and characterized by competition over the definition of "Russian" and the way Russia should achieve a genuine great-power status.

Since the mid-1980s, and particularly after the dissolution of the USSR, different political currents and ideologies have clashed over what the definition of Russian identity

---

[105] James H. Billington, "The Search for a Modern Russian Identity," Bulletin of the American Academy of Arts and Sciences, Vol. 45, No. 4 (Jan., 1992), 34, http://www.jstor.org/stable/3824597, Accessed: 05/08/2012.

[106] Ibid.

and how Russia's foreign policy and interactions with the post–Cold War international system should be. At the turn of the century, Gorbachev and Yeltsin's policies aiming at integration with the West, were replaced by an independent approach of Putin's, once they confronted domestic opposition and foreign skepticism. This independent foreign-policy approach, distinct from those of the liberal capitalist West, is basically a product of the Russian elite's "deep-seated consensus" over the identity of Russia as a state and the nature of international relations.[107] The despair, defiance, and existential crisis experienced by the Russians with the collapse of communism and unprecedented strategic contraction, played an important role in the strengthening of anti-Western ideas and a unique and independent Russian way.[108]

The mainstream of political thought since mid-1800s in Russia has always been the Slavophile. Richard Pipes points out that the Slavophile has become the most pivotal current in Russian intellectual history.[109] The "Slavophile theory" was born as a reaction to German thinkers' dismissal of the contributions of the Slavs to the advance of civilization and their relegation of Slavs to the category of "unhistoric nations."[110] This fueled a big controversy within the Russian intelligentsia in the late 1830s, Richard Pipes asserts.[111] He notes that in 1836, Peter Chaadaev argued, in line with German thinkers, that Russia did not contribute to the advance of civilization at all, by adding that it was a 'historic swampland' without a past and future. To Chaadaev, this was so because Russia had inherited Christianity from a "polluted source," Byzantium, which led to its isolation from the West. Ultimately, his essay started a controversy that has never ceased since then and split the Russian intelligentsia in two: Slavophiles and Westernizers.[112]

---

[107] Mankoff, *The Return of Great Power Politics*, 11.

[108] Erickson, *Russia Will Not Be Trifled*, 242.

[109] Pipes, *Russia Under the Old Regime*, 267.

[110] Ibid., 265.

[111] Ibid., 265.

[112] Ibid., 266.

"According to the Slavophile theory the fundamental difference between Russia and the West were traceable to religion."[113] Slavophiles believed that Orthodoxy remained devoted to true Christian ideals, while Western Christianity was influenced by the classical cultures, rationalism, and excessive pride. The collective faith and wisdom of the flock drove its strength, and unlike the West's individualistic and legalistic mind, "[the] communal spirit formed the quintessential feature of Russian national character and provided the basis of all Russian institutions." [114] Above all, the fantastic idealization of the past led Slavophiles to conclude that Russia was the country of the future, destined to abolish the chains around the neck of mankind and eliminate all political and class conflicts. [115]

On the other hand, there was no unity among the opponents of the Slavophiles, except rejection of their ideas as ignorant and utopian. Pipes points out that "they [anti-Slavophiles] did not deny that Russia was different from the West, but they explained this difference by her backwardness rather than uniqueness."[116] They were just adopting the view that Russia needed to get rid of its past and traditions and take a new way, the Western way.

During the years following the disintegration of the USSR, the historical contest between Slavophiles and Westernizers over Russian identity transformed into a debate between nationalists, Eurasianists, and Westernizers.

As a consequence of social and economic bankruptcy toward the end of the Soviet era, the pro-Western camp raised its voice and called for reform and regeneration that would transform Russia into a liberal democratic state and a member of the free world. Many of them favored cooperation with the West, adherence to international norms, and integration with Western institutions. To them, the journey towards becoming a part of Western civilization that started with the reforms of Peter and was interrupted by the Bolshevik Revolution and totalitarian rule of Stalin should be resumed and completed.

---

[113] Ibid., 267.
[114] Ibid., 267.
[115] Ibid., 268.
[116] Ibid., 268.

Gorbachev and Yeltsin were strong adherents of the Westernization of policies and the belief that Russia is historically and culturally a European power that will eventually integrate into the West. Former prime ministers Yegor Gaidar and Sergei Krienko and foreign minister Andrey Kozyrev were also prominent members of the Westernist camp. However, the optimism and support to Westernizers withered away as Yeltsin failed to jumpstart the Russian economy and national pride. Nevertheless, as Mankoff emphasizes, liberal and Westernist ideas have still been represented well among the Russian intelligentsia and garner support from many educated Russians.[117] And they influence, particularly, the economic policies of Russia and its interactions with the global economic system.

A prominent thinker in Westernizer camp and a career military-intelligence officer, Dmitri Trenin, argues that Russia is both historically and culturally part of Europe and its survival depends on its ability to transform itself and embrace Western liberal democratic values. To him, Russia should focus on economic opportunity, growth, and development, and abandon its great-power fantasies. Germany and Japan, in the post–World War II era, should set the example for Russian thinkers and policymakers looking for a strategy in the 21st century, according to Trenin.[118]

The implications of the collapse of the Soviet Union were substantial; failure of social and economic policies and ongoing existential crisis led to the dissolution of the immediate optimism and appetite for Westernization, and to the consolidation of nationalist currents. Russian nationalism, Jeffrey Mankoff notes, is a loose collection of groups and activist that are prone to racial policies. They usually prefer "a smaller and more homogenous Russia," in a kind of "fortress Russia" mentality, rather than a larger and integrated Russia within the post-Soviet space. Expansionism does not take precedence in their agenda. Their policies aim at opposing Chinese immigrants to the Russian Far East and Muslim Republics to the south, in rather xenophobic tones. The Movement Against Illegal Immigration, (*Dvizhenie protivv nelegal'noi immigratsii*, DPNI) is the most popular nationalist political organization, conveying discontent and

---

[117] Mankoff, *The Return of Great Power Politics*, 72.

[118] Ibid., 73.

anxiety about the future among ethnic Russians.[119] Russian nationalists, who are preoccupied with immigration issues and the former Muslim Republics of the USSR, get along well with the West and do not reject cooperation between Russia and the West.

To Eurasianists, Mankoff points out, "Russia's fundamental identity and hence foreign policy priorities, are linked to its geographical position at the crossroads between Europe and Asia."[120] Eurasianism encompasses different tones on a spectrum of political approaches: aggressive and imperial on one end and softer, synthesizing the views of Westernizers and Slavophiles in a third way, on the other end. Mankoff asserts that they typically attempt to justify their aggressiveness by citing Zbigniew Brezinski's formulation for the post–Cold War international order: a "grand chessboard."[121] Eurasianists imagine a Russia comprising the former Soviet space. built upon a unique Eurasian civilization. They see the West as a natural geopolitical competitor.[122]

Since the Primakov era, however, a balanced compromise among these ideas, what is called centrism, has shaped Moscow's foreign policy. Yevgeny Primakov, serving as foreign minister to Yeltsin between 1996 and 1998, pursued a balanced foreign-policy course aimed at restoration of Russia as a leading power. He was not anti-Western, yet rejected a subservient relationship to the West. He stressed the image of Russia as a great power and the need to design a foreign policy centering on this core idea. In this regard, Primakov offered four foreign policy tasks: First, "creating external conditions conducive to strengthening the country's territorial integrity;" second, "strengthening processes of reintegration, especially in the economy, in the former USSR;" third, "settling regional and interethnic conflicts in the CIS and former Yugoslavia," and last, preventing the creation of new areas of tension and proliferation of WMDs.[123] Remembering the priorities of Russian foreign policy today, articulated in what some have termed as "the Medvedev doctrine," there are many similarities among

---

[119] Ibid., 64–5.

[120] Ibid., 64.

[121] Ibid., 65.

[122] Ibid., 65–7.

[123] Donaldson and Nogee, *Changing Systems, Enduring Interest,* 116.

the foreign policy outlooks of these periods. Thus, it is fair to argue that many tendencies in Russian foreign policy attributed to Vladimir Putin constitute continuity since the mid-1990s.[124] Mankoff suggests, "Less an ideological movement than an attempt to synthesize the competing priorities of the other three camps . . . Russian centrism has remained the dominant approach since around 1993–1994, precisely because of its success in appealing to a broad constituency among the elite."[125] In line with the centrist tendency, different groups have united over the notion that Russia is an independent great power and should play a pivotal role in world affairs.[126] Centrism reflects, thus, a compromise over the debate about whether Russia is European or Asian, and to which civilization it belongs.

Centrism provides a geopolitical view combining Eurasians' emphasis on Russia's regional and global leading role and Westernizers' suggestion of non-confrontational, productive relations with the West. It is the manifestation of the consensus over Russian identity as a result of a thorny process. Centrists favor a foreign policy balancing the attention devoted to interests and obligations in the West and the East. While they support Russia's central, leading role in the former Soviet space, they avoid direct confrontation with the U.S. and Europe. On the other hand, good relations with the West, which they see essential for economic progress, should not lead them to disregard their hinterland, Asia. According to what centrists called the "multivectoral approach to foreign policy," Russia should balance its efforts toward the West and its neighbors in Central and East Asia and avoid getting into a position that would necessitate making a selection between them. Overall, Russia's ongoing close relations with China (its decision to sell high-tech weapons for instance) and Iran (such as contributions to its nuclear program, despite the objections of the West), and its emphasis

---

[124] Mankoff, *The Return of Great Power Politics*, 28.

[125] Ibid., 63.

[126] Ibid., 63.

on CIS countries in recent foreign-policy documents—simultaneously its efforts to normalize relations with West—could be considered within the context of this multivectoral approach.[127]

Russia has been cautious in its relations with the West and avoided committing to a full-scale security integration that will subordinate it to the U.S. or EU. It favors arrangements among great powers that enable it to have equal voice, like the UN Security Council. Despite its full support to the U.S. after the September 11 attacks, for instance, Russia insisted on a partnership that would be based on equality. Even some centrists tilted toward Westernizers, favoring integration with the EU and cooperation with the U.S., suggesting that this happen in a way that allows Russia to protect its identity and historical features.[128]

In sum, centrism is a manifestation of compromise over the question of what Russian identity is. It comprises features of the nationalist, Eurasianist, and Westernist currents. In Moscow's foreign-policy design since Primakov's term, centrism, a rational and balanced compromise of Russian political and strategic currents, has been the main approach of Russian foreign policy. With regard to cooperation between Russia and the West, more specifically between Russia and NATO, centrism provides many opportunities, since it favors a long-term rapprochement between Russia and the West, and aims for a productive, non-confrontational relationship.

E. RELIGION

Russia's denominational choice had a deep impact on its identity. Orthodoxy distanced Russia's fate from the West and led to quite a distinct social character. After a breakup with religion during the Soviet era, Russia has enjoyed a religious revival since Gorbachev. Directly and indirectly, Orthodox Christianity contributed to Russia's lonely player image and influenced how it sees itself and world politics. It has led to Russia's isolation from Western civilization and contributed to its lagging behind the social and economic progress experienced by the West.

---

[127] Ibid., 68.

[128] Ibid., 70.

At the end of 10th century, Prince Vladimir of Kiev embraced Eastern Christianity under the influence of Constantinople and its Patriarch.[129] Constantinople's political and economic superiority over Rome, its geographical proximity, emissaries sent from Hagia Sofia, and commercial activity with Byzantine merchants were important factors behind Orthodox belief's expansion into Russian lands. Among scholars studying Russian identity, the consequences of this marriage of Russia and Orthodox Christianity have commanded more attention than the reasons for its happening. It can be argued that Orthodoxy is one of the factors alienating Russia from the West. Richard Pipes writes, "The fact that Russia received its Christianity from Byzantium rather than from the West had the most profound consequences for the entire course of Russia's historic development."[130] As a result of the decision of Prince Vladimir, Russia became separated from the mainstream of Christianity. Lately and perhaps most importantly, for instance, during the Enlightenment age and industrial revolution, which led to civilizational leaps in the West, while Western religious leaders were seeking ways to accommodate faith to science and the needs of society, the Russian patriarchy was moving in the opposite direction, "towards renunciation, mysticism, hypnosis, and ecstasy."[131]

Moscow's inheritance of Orthodox leadership from Byzantium after the conquest of Constantinople by the Ottomans had serious impacts on the Russian psyche and identity. In 1589, the Russian church became autocephalous, and the Moscow patriarchy was established. From this time on, the Church's influence in society increased considerably. In the 16th century, Moscow was the only large kingdom in support of this eastern Christianity, which made it the target of assaults by Catholicism and Islam. As a consequence the Russian Church became increasingly intolerant. Russia felt lonelier than even before; after its self-survival from the Mongol–Tatar domination, its assumption of

---

[129] Pipes, *Russia Under the Old Regime*, 221.

[130] Ibid., 223.

[131] Ibid., 222.

Orthodox leadership nurtured its ego and self-appreciation even more. This was another factor isolating Russia from its neighbors and the West and establishing a leadership role into the Russian subconscious.[132]

The Orthodox Church has never had a power and authority equivalent to the Catholic Church in the West. The state's authority always eclipsed their influence and power. Though it enjoyed a golden age during Mongol domination, when it was granted protection and exemption from tribute and taxes, it has never accumulated considerable wealth and was never centrally controlled, as the Catholic Church was in Western Europe. Even so, it had semi-autonomy and institutional identity until Peter the Great changed it, subjugating it entirely to the state, abolishing the patriarchate, and transforming it into a branch of state administration. He deprived it of many of its privileges and incomes as well. On the other hand, Peter and his successors merely saw the church as an essential component of Russianness and used it as a tool for exerting a homogenization policy by forcing non-Orthodox people under their rule to adopt Orthodoxy. As a result, from its introduction to the end of the tsarist era, to a decreasing degree but in an increasingly lasting way, a close connection was formed between Russianness and Orthodoxy.[133]

The Bolshevik Revolution, and subsequently almost a century-long experience with socialism, created a wedge between Russianness and Orthodoxy. In the Soviet era, anti-church policies and the suppression of clergy, common believers, and any symbol of religion in society, art, and culture led to a diminishing influence of religion in Russian identity. That is not to say Soviet leaders never resorted to religious motives. From time to time, when circumstances necessitated, such as during World War II, when patriotic feelings needed to be stirred, this general approach against religion was violated by

---

[132] Ibid., 223.

[133] Simon Franklin, "Identity and Religion" in Simon Franklin and Emma Widdis (eds) National Identity in Russian Culture: an Introduction, (Cambridge: Cambridge University Press, 2004): 95–104 cited in Tobias Van Treeck, "Faith in Russia? Exploring National Identity Discourses on Russian Belonging and the Role of Religion,"(Master's Thesis, University of Tampere, 2009).

Soviet leaders. However, it would be fair to say that during the Soviet era, the Orthodox Church's influence on society and Russian identity reduced remarkably, if not vanished entirely.[134]

With *glasnost* and *perestroika,* the anti-religious policies of the Soviet era were amended and a religious regeneration was introduced for Russian people. Religious institutions were revitalized and the Orthodox Church began to reconstitute its influence. While the popularity of Orthodoxy was reinstated, the number of atheists decreased remarkably in the post-Soviet period. What is widely called a "religious revival," arguably, could be associated also with economic, social, and political collapse and wounded national pride. It was what the nation needed in a time of serious crises or when an existential threat appeared.

To conclude, Orthodoxy is one of the key elements of contemporary Russian identity. It also is a factor in Russian development of an identity distinct from Western Europe. Its unchanging subservience to state and the way it enhanced submission instead of tolerance in society contributed to the authoritarian political culture in Russia. Since 1453, when Russia became the leading and almost the only representative of Orthodox states, the sense of insecurity and self-appreciation in Russian psyche has consolidated. The denominational choice of Russia has contributed to its lonely player image and the realist way it conceptualizes international politics. It has led to Russia's isolation from Western civilization and lagging behind the social and economic progress of the West.

F. CONCLUSION

Russian foreign policy is the product of the combination of historical, cultural, religious, and geopolitical factors with the rational choices of the Russian elite and people. From rule of the tsars and general secretaries of the Communist Party to Orthodoxy, and from its Asian and European cultural heritage to geographic and geopolitical realities, many elements influence the foreign policy designs of Kremlin. These realities help scholars better understand Russia's foreign-policy behavior and help them make projections about the future decisions and moves of Russia.

---

[134] Ibid., 104.

Russia's geographic and geopolitical realities help explain its ever-existing insecurity and the rationale behind its expansionist behavior, and clarify Russia's contemporary emphasis on CIS countries and overreaction to NATO enlargement. The post–Cold War world order has given way to the emergence of new powers around Russia, leaving it in an unprecedented position, in which it is surrounded by political entities that are highly dynamic and increasingly powerful. This brand-new geopolitical setting of the 21st century forces Russia to cooperate both with the West and its Asian neighbors, avoiding confrontation while trying to regenerate its economy and domestic order.

The Russian identity crisis that reemerged after the break-up of the Soviet Union seems to have settled down with a sort of agreement on centrism, finding a compromise between its autocratic culture and democratic future, its nostalgia for the imperial past and the attractions of the West, and its Asian and European heritages. The religious revival enjoyed in Russia since *Perestroika* contributed to this compromise as well, considering it has been an essential element of its identity. The historical debate over Russian identity between Slavophiles and Westernizers was transformed into one among nationalists, Eurasianists, and Westernizers. The Russian elite, after a short pro-Western experience, seemingly agreed on a civic identity encompassing all the people within the borders of Russia and compromising the contesting views of the intelligentsia. And notably, it managed to devise a foreign policy in conformity with its agreed-upon identity reflecting centrism, a combination of the views of Eurasianists and Westernizers.

To conclude, both geographic and geopolitical realities and an agreed-upon identity have led Russia to design a balanced foreign policy, which, in many respects, favors cooperative, non-confrontational relations with the West and its Asian neighbors, and praises its leading role in the former Soviet space and global affairs.

IV. VLADIMIR PUTIN AND RUSSIAN FOREIGN POLICY IN THE TWENTY-FIRST CENTURY

Russia's foreign policy outlook has changed considerably and become increasingly assertive during the presidency of Vladimir Putin and his political ally Dmitri Medvedev. The allegedly deterioration of the relations between Russia and the West also coincided with Putin's term in the Kremlin. Many have blamed Putin for the growingly troubled relations between the West and Russia. Among those things that have brought him a sinister reputation, a status of "reviled figure," in Western capitals and Western media, were the assassinations of such public figures as Andrei Kozlov, deputy chairman of Russia's central Bank, and Anna Politkovskaya, a pioneering journalist known for her criticism to the war in Chechnya and Putin's increasing power in Russia, in 2006, the Kremlin's harsh reaction to color revolutions in former Soviet space, nationalization of some companies in the energy sector, gas cutoffs, overt and covert support to the Iranian nuclear program, suspension of the Conventional Forces in Europe (CFE) Treaty, opposition to Western policies regarding Kosovo, and the invasion of Georgia.[135] What has been the role of Vladimir Putin in this changing, assertive outlook in the Russian foreign policy? Is he an obstacle to the improvement of relations with the West, particularly with NATO? In the following section, the change in Russian foreign policy and Vladimir Putin's impact on this change will be analyzed.

A. RUSSIA'S ASSERTIVE FOREIGN POLICY IN THE TWENTY-FIRST CENTURY

Although it was not fundamental, the change in Russia's foreign-policy outlook and Moscow's alleged assertiveness is caused by two main group of factors, internal and external. Quite interrelated internal factors include Russia's economic consolidation in the last decade and the Russian elite's strengthening consensus over Russian identity and the international role and goals of Russia. On the other hand, there are three main external factors influencing Russian foreign policy: first, the West's failure to

---

[135] Mankoff, *The Return of Great Power Politics*, 25.

accommodate Russia; second, transnational threats in the post–September 11 security environment, and last, a new geopolitical setting with the emergence of new political and economic powers around Russia.

1.   Internal Factors

As the primary internal factor in this change, Russian economic performance in 21st century has been substantial. In almost two decades, economic conditions in Russia have changed dramatically. Since 1999, the GDP has grown about 7 percent annually. The overall size of the economy enlarged more than six times in current dollars. From 2000 to 2005, the annual income of Russian people grew 26 percent. Russia received substantial direct foreign investment during those years. The performance was basically because of the rise of the global energy prices in 2008; however, government made some effort to decrease reliance on energy exports.[136]

The change in Putin's approach to foreign-policy issues coincides with the change in Russia's economic conditions. As Russian economic strength rose, its international political influence grew as well. This process also consolidated Putin's domestic political power.[137] To put it in other words Russia's global and regional political assertiveness strengthened as the economy and Putin's domestic powerbase consolidated.

The amelioration in the economy led to the restoration of Russian national pride and self-confidence. Until the second term of Putin, particularly until the rise of global energy prices in 2008, Russia's foreign policy remained "passive" and "reactive." At first, Putin was rather obedient to Western policies, even in the case of the integration of Baltic States in NATO. However, Russia's newfound energy wealth has led to a sense of independence and power in Moscow and helped resurrect its leadership character. Therefore, the changes in Russian foreign policy outlook in the second term of Putin has

---

[136] Andrei P. Tsygankov, "Russia's Foreign Policy," in After Putin's Russia: Past Imperfect Future Uncertain, ed. Stephen K. Wegren and Dale R. Herspring (Lanham, MD, Rowman & Littlefield Publishers, 2009), 224.

[137] Donaldson and Nogee, *Changing Systems, Enduring Interest,* 340.

not much to do with his personality; rather they are the outcome of Russia's stronger position in the international arena, originating mostly from the economic recovery. [138]

With the help of the economic recovery, domestic conditions in Russia also improved. The Russian elite and people are feeling more confident in defining the role of Russia. Two major political ideologies conflicted in this regard: Atlanticism and Eurasianism. The liberal and democratic-minded supporters of Atlanticism were defending the view of absolute integration with the West by adopting the ideas and institutions of it, while Eurasianists put emphasis on the unique identity of Russia, comprising both Western and Asian features. After oscillating between Atlanticism and Eurasianism, the political elite consensus embraced the blend of these two political ideologies, called centrism. The supporters of this ideology admit the superiority of and the need to tilt toward Western civilization, while attributing to Russia a great power role in international affairs, particularly in the former Soviet space. In this sense, Jeffrey Mankoff asserts "Foreign policy under Putin achieved a kind of balance between the prescriptions of the Eurasianists and the liberal Atlanticists."[139]

This consensus has provided legitimacy and political support for Vladimir Putin to embrace a more assertive foreign policy. The head of the Center for International Security and the Institute for International Economy and International Relationships of the Russian Academy of Sciences, Alexei Arbatov, pointed out in 1994 that "There is an overwhelming consensus on the main goal of strategic and national security: that Russia should remain one of the world's great powers."[140] The strategic design pursued by Vladimir Putin has been a reflection of this consensus among the Russian elite concerning the nature of international relations and identity of Russia as a state. Putin, overall, just made some small touches and refashioned a foreign policy based on the general strategic consensus since the mid-1990s.[141]

---

[138] Mankoff, *The Return of Great Power Politics*, 24.

[139] Ibid., 82.

[140] Alexei G. Arbatov, "Russian National Interests," cited in Mankoff, *The Return of Great Power Politics*, 20.

[141] Mankoff, *The Return of Great Power Politics*, 11–2.

Actually the tide of Westernism in Russian politics started to change in the midst of the Yeltsin era. Even Yeltsin himself changed his pro-Western outlook toward the end of his term in office. Mankoff asserts, "The roots of (Russia's) estrangement" from the West "stretch further back, into the Yeltsin years (or beyond)." He reminds the reader of the criticism against Yeltsin because of his lapse from pro-Western foreign policy and his anti-democratic practices after a "brief flirtation" with the West in the beginning of 1990s.[142]

In foreign-policy terms, this early change came as a reaction to two fundamental frustrations of Russian elites and masses. The first was Russia's increasing subordination to the West and loss of national pride. Second was frustration over deteriorating domestic economic and social conditions, despite the hopeful rhetoric of pro-Western politicians regarding the virtues and benefits of democracy and a liberal economy.

In particular, during the Andrey Kozyrev's term as Russian foreign minister, between 1991 and 1996, developments disturbed the elite and public opinion. The perception that Kozyrev was kowtowing to the West without gaining anything in return sparked tremendous criticism among the elite and common people. For many, Kozyrev's submissive and passive approach was humiliating and undermined the international image and prestige of Russia. The Russian elite, who associated their country with imperial glories and a global power role, rejected the foreign-policy outlook under Kozyrev, no matter what the prospects of pursuing such a policy.[143]

Even more influential in the growth of a general reaction against the pro-Western approach of the Yeltsin and Kozyrev were the deteriorating social and economic conditions of the country during the reforms of the early 1990s. In the mind of the Russian electorate, democracy increasingly came to be associated with poverty and instability. The idea of Westernization and integration with the West gradually lost its appeal in the mid-1990s.[144]

---

[142] Ibid., 19.

[143] Ibid., 28.

[144] Ibid., 29–31.

2. External Factors

In addition to internal factors, such external factors as the West's failure to accommodate Russia, the changing geopolitical settings around the periphery of Russia, and finally the new security environment after September 11 have contributed to the change in Russian foreign policy outlook at the turn of century, strengthening the anti-Western political ideologies in Russian political culture.

The primary external factor that helped change the course of Russian foreign policy toward centrism and end the romance with Westernism was the West's failure to accommodate Russia in the aftermath of the breakup of the USSR. The West continued to act in the zero-sum thinking mode of the Cold War. Notably, the West's frustrating response to Russia's requests for economic aid helped change the course of Russian foreign policy.[145]

> Initially," according to Andrei P. Tsygankov, a professor at San Francisco State University, "the country's leadership was hoping to develop a grand strategy by engaging Western nations, in particular the United States, in projects of common significance, such as counterterrorism and energy security. However, as the West turned its attention elsewhere [Asia-Pacific] and as Russia grew stronger, the Kremlin made important adjustments to its policy.[146]

On the other hand, NATO as the flag-carrying institution of the West's hegemony, under the leadership of the U.S., was late to respond effectively to the immediate needs of the post–Cold War era. It failed to carry out the necessary structural and doctrinal transformation, and remained between containing and integrating Russia. As much as did Russia's strategic insecurity, NATO's uncertainty about the course it should follow hindered the development of full-fledged cooperation between the West

---

[145] Donaldson and Nogee, *Changing Systems, Enduring Interest,* 113.
[146] Tsygankov, "Russia's Foreign Policy,"224.

and Russia. Over all, North Atlantic Cooperation failed to manage Russian–NATO relations effectively.[147]

At the turn of the millennium, there existed several dynamic political entities around the borders of the Russian Federation. To the west, NATO and the EU continually enlarged their physical borders and area of influence toward Russia's traditional sphere of interest. To the Southeast, China skyrocketed its economic and political power, and began to disseminate a political and economic sphere of interests toward Central Asia and the Russian Far East. Finally, India, to the south, consolidated its economic and technological power and rose as a candidate of the great-powers club. Thomas Graham, former Director of the Russian and Eurasian Affairs at the National Security Council during George W. Bush's presidency, points out that "For the first time since Russia emerged as a great European power three centuries ago, it is now surrounded beyond the former Soviet space by countries and regions that are more dynamic than it is, economically, demographically and geopolitically."[148] This dynamism has contributed to one of the most notable aspects of Russian identity, its deep-seated insecurity. It has reinforced the perception among the Russian elite that particularly pro-Western foreign policy is a kind of subordination to the wills of the West and NATO and severely undermines Russia's future. Russia's growing economic strength and the erosion of power, and accordingly, of hegemon status, of the United States, based on change in the unipolar character of the international system, has contributed to Russia's self-confidence and encouraged Russia to act more independently. Over all, geopolitical developments at the turn of the millennium have led Russia to pursue a more assertive and independent foreign policy rather than a submissive, single-faceted, pro-Western approach.

After September 11, Moscow has been particularly concerned about the destabilization stemming from the U.S. strategy of global regime change. Three factors have concerned decision makers in the Kremlin: First, a possible color revolution, similar to those in Ukraine and Georgia; second, encirclement by pro-American regimes and

---

[147] Mankoff, *The Return of Great Power Politics*, 29.

[148] Thomas Graham, "Putin the Sequel," American Interest Magazine, Vol. 7, Nu. 4, March/April 2012.

NATO enlargement, which contributes to its sense of strategic insecurity; and finally, increasing radicalization of Islam, caused by the U.S.'s isolation of moderate Muslims.[149]

In the aftermath of September 11, radical Islamic terrorism became the predominant threat to any political entity of the era. "Russia [as well,] felt vulnerable to [the] radicalization of Islam."[150] Concerned about developments in the Middle East and Northern Africa, recently Russia seem to follow a different track in responding the democratic awakening of the people of the Muslim world. For instance, Russia's stance against a military intervention in Syria is a reflection both of its demand for respectful treatment as a well-regarded member of the international community and global player, and also of Russia's concern for the spread of radical Islamist movements to its near-abroad, northern Caucasus, and Central Asian states. It is also Russia's concern that such a situation could lead to a Libya-like unilateral intervention by NATO in regions that have close proximity to its borders. Therefore, Putin asserts that the reaction of the West to the Russian–Chinese veto of the UNSC resolution is merely hysterical. And any attempt to bypass this may have dangerous consequences in the long run. It can damage the authority of the UN and the working of the international system.[151]

B.   IS PUTIN ANTI-WESTERN?

The image of Vladimir Putin has been pretty dark for a long time in the West. His third term in the presidency has further strengthened concerns about the future of the relationship between the West and Russia. Particularly, the euphoria enjoyed during the presidency of Medvedev seems to have disappeared. The "reset" that started during the presidency of Dmitri Medvedev, under the initiative of the U.S. president Barack Obama, has gone on the backburner since Putin assumed the presidency of the Russian Federation for the third time. Medvedev's more modern and positive image, which seemed to ease

---

[149] Tsygankov, "Russia's Foreign Policy," 224.

[150] Ibid., 224.

[151] Vladimir Putin, Russia and the changing world, RIA Novosti at 27/02/2012 10:49

tension after the dark days of the last two years of the Bush administration, was replaced by a new wave of concern and pessimism upon the third election of Putin.[152]

Many scholars and Western foreign ministries are quite concerned about the implications of Putin's absolute regaining of the reins again. The principal objective of this section is to analyze the presidency's influence on foreign-policy decisions and try to address the question of whether Vladimir Putin really is an obstacle to a closer partnership between NATO and Russia.

1. The Presidency's Influence in the Making of Foreign Policy

The presidency in the making of the Russian foreign policy is influential, but not to the extent that it was in the USSR. Mankoff asserts that the presidency holds the strings, particularly in the 21st century; the ministry of foreign affairs and parliament do not play a major role.[153] And he notes that Putin's Russia was not a monolith, despite the centralization of decision-making processes. To him Putin, could not establish a complete top-down foreign-policy mechanism. Even though he curbed the influence of the legislature and regional authorities, such actors as the large energy companies and security services kept playing important roles in the making of foreign policy. The greatest achievement of Putin's centralized foreign-policy mechanism has been the creation of a "coherent vision of the national interest," which can hardly be observed in the Yeltsin–Primakov years. Yeltsin was unsuccessful in coordinating the activities and foreign-policy goals of the Security Council, foreign ministry, and many bureaucratic actors.[154]

As compared with Boris Yeltsin, Vladimir Putin assigns greater importance to foreign policy and wants to be more influential in the designing of it, since he thinks that domestic and foreign policies are interrelated and complementary to each other. He took many of these powers with him when he assumed the position of prime minister.[155]

---

[152] Graham, *Putin the Sequel*.

[153] Mankoff, *The Return of Great Power Politics*, 54.

[154] Ibid., 55–6.

[155] Ibid., 54.

"While it makes sense to speak of a Kozyrev foreign policy or a Primakov foreign policy, the same does not hold for a Lavrov foreign policy . . ."[156] In short, Putin's direct impact on foreign policy is substantial, however, he has tried to act within the lines of the general consensus over the identity of the Russia and foreign-policy outlook and his decisions have reflected the popular and intellectual demands. Donaldson and Nogee points out "Russian foreign policy emerges from the interaction of decision makers representing a variety of personal and institutional perspectives and involved in the simultaneous resolution of a large number of domestic and foreign issues."[157]

2. **The Putin Administration**

It is hard to define Vladimir Putin's foreign policy approach as anti-Western. It is assertive, it is more independent, it has grandiose aspirations, but it is quite pragmatic and multi-faceted. It is the product of complex and interrelated processes, social and political necessities. To put it another way, Putin's approach to the West has been shaped by many factors, especially by the needs of Russia's international position. But, one thing unchanging in Putin's foreign policy views is his commitment to the restoration of Russia as a great power.[158] And many of the policies that have created the perception that Russian foreign policy has become anti-Western under Putin's leadership have been a result of this commitment. In fact, during his presidency, no fundamental change occurred in the foreign-policy orientation of Russia. As Donaldson and Nogee point out "Vladimir Putin pursued a pragmatic, cautious, and nuanced foreign policy that revealed no clear-cut orientations. It revealed a mix of Atlanticist and Eurasianist ('pragmatic nationalist') perspectives."[159] He has not committed Russia to a single approach in its relations to the outside world; it has become European in its affairs with Europe, it has been a "transcontinental strategic partner" in relations with the U.S., Asian and Eurasian in Asia, and watchfully "integrationist" in the CIS.[160]

---

[156] Ibid., 55.

[157] Donaldson and Nogee, *Changing Systems, Enduring Interest*, 108.

[158] Mankoff, *The Return of Great Power Politics*, 23.

[159] Donaldson and Nogee, *Changing Systems, Enduring Interest*, 340.

[160] Duncan, *Contemporary Russian Identity between East and West*, 293.

Although it is widely claimed to be rhetorical, Putin, on several occasions, has emphasized Russia's belonging to the Western civilization and its European identity, while many times he also mentioned Russia as a Eurasian power. This actually reflects the inner dilemmas of Russia regarding its identity and belonging. Eurasia, as a term, is well embraced by only two nations, Turkey and Russia, who share similarities in their dilemmas of belongingness and identity between the West and East. It is not wrong to argue in this regard that this is the manifestation of both Putin's awareness of the Asian roots of Russian culture and his aspirations towards achieving the civilizational level of the West. It also demonstrates his pragmatic way in foreign policy.

The Putin administrations' priority and focus in foreign policy is enhancing the influence and power of Russia in the former Soviet space and the international arena without harming productive working relations with the West. In economic terms particularly, Putin has pursued integration with the West by ignoring the Eurasianists' call for a regional focus within the CIS. In this sense, Putin personally insisted on supporting the war of the U.S. against terrorism in cooperation with NATO, despite the opposite views of his advisors.[161] Putin's biggest concern has been, in fact, to be treated as an equal partner, to be accepted with its unique identity.[162] These terms were tacitly accepted by the Obama administration. Speaking in Munich in February 2009, Vice President Joseph Biden announced a "reset" of U.S. policy toward Russia. This has ushered in a period of constructive and productive relations between the two countries.

It is valuable at this point to take a look at "sovereign democracy" (*suverenneaya demokratiya*), Moscow's unofficial ideology, and its originator, Vladislav Surkov. Surkov is the godfather of the notion of sovereign democracy. He has held onto his position in government since the first term of Putin and occupied the deputy prime minister position since 2011. He is one of the grey cardinals—behind the scenes actors—of the Putin administration. Even though the sovereign-democracy concept is ambiguous and controversial, it basically emphasizes the ultimate independence of Russia,

---

[161] Mankoff, *The Return of Great Power Politics*, 76–81.
[162] Trenin, Post-Imperium, 27.

particularly from the West. To this idea, Russia has to maintain its sovereign role and uniqueness in the international arena and reject any foreign influence that could destabilize its position. Even the father of the thought, Surkov is not against integration with the West, and does not consider himself an Eurasianist unless it does not turn out to be subordination. Unlike Eurasianists thinkers such as Alexander Dugin, who sees sovereignty in foreign policy as a means of balancing the West, Surkov promotes sovereignty as a way of having freedom of choice in foreign policy. For him, sovereignty is just for enabling Moscow room for maneuver in international affairs and freedom of action that will allow it to move along its own interests, independent of the influence of international organizations.[163]

On the other hand, Russia's foreign policy remained fundamentally the same during Putin's terms. The wind of change that dragged Russian foreign policy away from the pro-Western axis dates back to the era of Yevgeny Primakov, the successor of Kozyrev. Mankoff asserts that foundations of most of the foreign policies pursued by Putin was laid in Primakov's term as foreign minister, though Primakov and Putin were political rivals for the presidential nomination in 2000.[164]

Yevgeny Primakov, served as the foreign minister under Yeltsin between 1996 and 1998, pursuing a balanced foreign policy tilted toward restoration of Russia as a leading power. He was not anti-Western, yet rejected a subservient relationship to the West. He put emphasis on the image of Russia as a great power and the need to design a foreign policy centering on this core idea. Primakov promoted four foreign-policy tasks: first, "creating external conditions conducive to strengthening the country's territorial integrity;" second, "strengthening processes of reintegration, especially in the economy, in the former USSR;" third, "settling regional and interethnic conflicts in the CIS and former Yugoslavia," and last, preventing the creation of new areas of tension and proliferation of WMDs.[165] Remembering the priorities of Russian foreign policy today articulated in what some have termed as "the Medvedev doctrine," there are many

---

[163] Mankoff, *The Return of Great Power Politics*, 77–9.

[164] Ibid., 28.

[165] Donaldson and Nogee, *Changing Systems, Enduring Interest*, 116.

similarities among the foreign policy outlooks of those periods. Thus it is fair to argue that many tendencies in Russian foreign policy attributed to Vladimir Putin actually represent continuity since the mid-1990s.[166] Such notions as the creation of a multipolar world ruled by international law and Russia's interests in the former Soviet states have existed in Russian foreign-policy documents for two decades.[167]

3. Putin's Third Term

Putin's return to office generated deep concern in the Western capitals and media regarding the democratic future of Russia and its future ties with the West. Many claimed that this would bring an end to the reset in U.S.-Russia relations, wishing that Medvedev had stayed in office. However, it should be remembered that Medvedev was able to pursue the reset only with Putin's full, tacit approval.[168] Thomas Graham asserts,

> Even had Medvedev stayed on as President, the road ahead would have been rocky. But Putin's return exacerbates the situation, for he symbolizes the stark differences in values, interests and outlook that still divide Russia and the United States and feed the dark images of Russia that, rightly or wrongly, pervade the American political establishment.[169]

For sure there are many rightful concerns about the democratic future of Russia, considering the domestic non-democratic practices, bad management of elections, including allegations of ballot stuffing, and using state funds for the interests of the United Russia Party. It is not easy to argue that Russia's democratic future is bright, at least in the short run; however, considering Russia is still a middle-income developing country, its democratic and liberal economic performance is quite different from those countries in the same category. To Andrei Shleifer and Daniel Treisman, the Western media and politicians have mostly tended to view and describe Russia as a collapsed and evil state inhabited by criminals and threatening other countries with multiple contagions rather than as a middle-income country struggling to

---

[166] Mankoff, *The Return of Great Power Politics*, 28.

[167] Ibid., 29–31.

[168] Graham, *Putin the Sequel*.

[169] Ibid.

overcome its Communist past and deep-rooted Communist legacy and find its place in the international system.[170] All democracies in this range have troubles such as corruption, a politicized judiciary, censorship of the press, and income inequality. In this respect, Russia is a normal country.[171] It cannot be argued that Russia is in the way of being a capitalist, liberal-democratic country, but it is obvious that it is neither in the way of becoming a dictatorship. Vladimir Putin himself is not the reason of the problems facing Russia today; they stem from structural and deep-rooted factors.

It is highly likely that "A new Putin presidency will undoubtedly occasionally contain harsh rhetoric and recriminations against the West, aimed in part at impressing a domestic audience."[172] Yet, this is not to say that Putin fundamentally and categorically against the West.

Establishment of civilian control over the military in the last decade and, recently, establishment of a new relatively liberal and less corrupt cabinet, along with Russia's entry into the World Trade Organization (WTO), are positive developments for the democratic future of Russia and support the argument that Putin is not anti-Western.

This new liberality has surprised everyone dealing with Russian politics.

> The old cabinet was stacked with ministers considered highly corrupt, including former KGB officers and Putin cronies from his days in the St. Petersburg city government. With a couple of exceptions, they are all gone. Despite some suggestions that the new cabinet represents Putin's attempt to solidify his control over the new government, the group is in fact, dominated by liberal technocrats.[173]

Putin's ousting of corrupt politicians and his former KGB cronies can assist Russian progress toward liberal democracy. On the other hand, just as with China a

---

[170] Andrei Shleifer and Daniel Treisman "A Normal Country," *Foreign Affairs,* Mar/April 2004. Vol. 83, Iss. 2, 20.

[171] Ibid., 22.

[172] Philip Hanson, James Nixey, Lilia Shevtsova and Andrew Wood, Conclusion to *"Putin Again: Implications for Russia and the West,"* Chatham House Report, February 2012

[173] Anders Åslund, Russia's Surprisingly Liberal New Cabinet, Foreign Policy Magazine, 21 May 2012, http://www foreignpolicy.com/articles/2012/05/21/russia_s_surprisingly_liberal_new_cabinet.

decade ago, WTO membership should press Russia to compete more openly and fairly in world markets and to abide more closely by international trade rules.[174]

To conclude, the Putin administration is not responsible for Russia's assertive foreign policy in the 21st century. The change and increasing assertiveness not only started before Putin's rise to the office, it is also the product of some internal and external factors. While Russia's economic consolidation in the last decade, along with the Russian elite's strengthening consensus over Russian identity and the international role and goals of Russia, constitute internal factors, external factors are the West's failure to accommodate Russia, transnational threats of the post–September 11 security environment, and a new geopolitical setting with the emergence of new political and economic powers around Russia. Putin himself has never been anti-Western during his presidency. He is well aware of the need for the modernization of Russia's political and economic systems and appreciates the achievements in Westernization since Peter the Great. Considering the popular and elite demand for Russia's great power status and prestigious position in international affairs, his assertive and sometimes harsh rhetoric against the Western powers make sense.

Putin's years in the presidency also coincide with the emergence of dynamic actors around the periphery of Russia. While China, India, and Southeast Asian countries experienced substantial economic and political consolidation, NATO and the EU enlarged their borders toward Russia's immediate neighborhood. The combination of enhanced strategic insecurity and increasing economic and political power has led the Putin administration to develop a more independent and assertive foreign policy, placing priorities first on restoring the international prestige of Russia and then on rebuilding its influence on former Soviet countries in Eastern Europe and Central Asia. Therefore, it is wrong to argue that Putin's policies were either absolutely pro- or purely anti-Western.[175] Putin has sought to maintain ties and partnerships with the West while trying to avoid a subservient position.

---

[174] *Russia and the West*, The Economist, 16 June 2012, http://www.economist.com/node/21556955

[175] Donaldson and Nogee, *Changing Systems, Enduring Interest,* 341.

V. COOPERATIVE SECURITY AND THE NATO-RUSSIA RELATIONS

Scholars mostly agree on three main factors inhibiting mutual positive approaches and limiting the improvement of cooperation at a certain level. They are the distinction between Russian and Western identity, the Russian political culture's authoritarian tendencies, and the legacy of old hatreds, namely deep-seated reciprocal distrust. As observed chapters III and IV, these obstacles can be surmounted. Despite the abundance of obstacles, both sides have been aware of their common interests and challenges. After the Cold War, and particularly September 11, 2001, new security challenges created a common ground and helped bridge the gap between the two major actors in global politics. Throughout this process, the cooperative security concept contributed a lot to the amelioration of relations and overcoming of well-known impediments. Beginning with the 1970s, the realist perspective of old enemies has been gradually replaced by the constructive approaches of parties. This change will be analyzed by discussing why and how the cooperative-security concept has fostered relations, and how the relations evolved within the framework of this concept, with the help of its institutions.

In short, this chapter seeks to explore the prospects of a strategic partnership and closer relations liberated from the shadow of distrust. After conceptually analyzing the cooperative-security concept and its benefits, as a framework for NATO–Russian relations, it will provide a review of the implementation of the concept—its birth and development—in a historical perspective, focusing on the late Cold War, post–Cold War, and post–September 11 eras.

A. COLLECTIVE DEFENSE, COLLECTIVE SECURITY, AND COOPERATIVE SECURITY

The mutual misperceptions about the intentions of policy and strategy fuel mistrust on each side of the old east west divide in the past two decades. This fact is accordingly the major source of conflict and sometimes 'undesirable competition' in international relations. Cooperation in this sense is invaluable, since it helps persuade parties that some actions are fueled by their reciprocal insecurity, not by "greed" and helps reduce the possibility of conflict. Lionel Ponsard asserts that misperceptions and mutual suspicion in an anarchic system can damage security and stability, no matter how much peaceful intentions the participants of the system have. He suggests a "legal and diplomatic means to keep eye on each other" as the only way to alleviate the security dilemma and prevent undesired competition.[176] There are two dimensions to this: first, keeping eye on each other within organizations and institutions, and second between states or organizations, through cooperative arrangements or bilateral cooperative interactions. Three cooperative concepts, in this sense, have shaped NATO as a security organization and in its relations with other entities.

Concepts of collective defense, collective security, and cooperative security are all concepts in which states choose to cooperate in various degrees of interdependency and partnership for their own interest. They are also the interrelated and complementary conceptual pillars of NATO on which its structure and policies are built. Despite being blurred, there are stark differences between what they mean and what their definitions are. Before examining how and why cooperative security provides the most suitable context for the NATO-Russia relations, their differences should be understood.

Collective-security and -defense concepts are the creations of 20th-century efforts to configure a system of stability and peace with roots in the 18th and 19th centuries. They aim to overcome the negative consequences of the anarchic character of the international system and counterweighting and deterring an over-strengthened enemy. "Both concepts imply a long–term, formal commitment between groups of states to protect the security interests of individual members within their common spheres."[177] Collective security aims to restore and maintain peace via multilateral commitments and arrangements to limit, deter, or destroy an aggression by the joint action of the all member states. The strongest supporter of this concept was President Woodrow Wilson, It favors collective reaction against a potential aggressor and a collective protection guarantee for the potential victim of an aggression, to encourage participation and deter

---

[176] Ponsard, *Bridging the Gap*, 117–8.

[177] Richard Cohen, *Cooperative Security: Individual Security to International Stability,* George C. Marshall European Center for Security Studies, 2001, 5.

aggressors. In this regard, it is an inward-looking concept, as it aims to achieve security within the states. A group of states pledges to defend each other in case of an attack or aggression within the group, the first example of which in history is the League of Nations.[178] Lionel Ponsard claims that, by building confidence and promoting cooperation, collective security systems reduce the possibility of security dilemmas, promote stability, and help establish a middle course between global governance and international anarchy.[179]

In contrast to collective security, collective defense systems, a product of the Second World War and Cold War, are outward looking and based on the pledge of a group of states to defend each other from external "predetermined" threats and enemies.[180] "It implies a determinate structure for a determinate purpose, and requires, although not always named, a determinate foe."[181]

> Because an alliance, or collective defense pact, is an instrument of states cooperating to seek security from external threats posed by others, one of its chief preoccupations is achieving a favorable, or at least acceptable, balance of power as a means of deterring war or hedging against its outbreak.[182]

This can clearly be observed in the North Atlantic Treaty's Article 5: "The Parties agree that an armed attack against one or more of them in Europe or North America shall be considered an attack against them all . . . "[183] In its 1991 strategic concept, also it is clearly identified that "the security of all Allies is indivisible: an attack to one is an attack to all."[184]

The cooperative-security concept, on the other hand, has become popular since the beginning of the 1990s. In a modern sense, its roots go back to the 1970s, to the Cold

---

[178] Ponsard, *Bridging the Gap*, 123.

[179] Ibid., 124.

[180] Ibid., 124.

[181] Ibid., 124.

[182] Yost, *NATO Transformed*, 7.

[183] North Atlantic Treaty, para. 5.

[184] North Atlantic Council, Strategic Concept, November 7, 1991, par.37.

War between the United States and Soviet Union.[185] "It has been generally used to describe a more peaceful, but rather idealistic, approach to security through increased international harmony and cooperation."[186] Cooperative security is based on the assumption that uncertainty about each other's intentions generates insecurity among states. Thus, it aims to regulate interstate attitudes via common norms, rules, and standards that might otherwise cause misperceptions and misleading interpretations. While collective security and defense systems seek to deter and defeat threats and require preparations for such, cooperative-security systems seek to prevent threats before they originate.[187] In this sense, Cohen asserts, "it appeared to offer an escape from narrow Cold War "zero-sum" strategies in to the broad sunlit vistas of international peace and harmony."[188]

Accordingly, Richard Cohen's model for cooperative security, "Cooperative Security: The Four Rings," based on the notion of widening concentric rings, may help explain the discrepancies in the three security concepts. To him,

> "Cooperative Security is a strategic system which forms around a nucleus of liberal democratic states linked together in a network of formal or informal alliances and institutions characterized by shared values and practical and transparent economic, political, and defense cooperation. In a Cooperative Security system, individual states' national security objectives are linked by four reinforcing rings of security: Ring One: Individual Security (Promoting and protecting human rights within their own boundaries and further afield), Ring Two: Collective Security (Maintaining peace and stability within their common space), Ring Three: Collective Defense (Mutual protection against outside aggression, Ring Four: Promoting Stability (Actively promoting stability in other areas where conflict could threaten their shared security, using political, informational, economic, and, if necessary, military means)."[189]

---

[185] Catherine M. Kelleher, *"Cooperative Security in Europe: New Wine, New Bottles, "* CISSM Working Paper, 13April 2012, Accessed on 4 June 2012, http://www.cissm.umd.edu/papers/files/cooperative_security_in_europenew_wine_new_bottles_041312.pdf.

[186] Cohen, *Individual Security to International Stability*, 1.

[187] Ponsard, *Bridging the Gap*, 125–6.

[188] Cohen, *Individual Security to International Stability*, 3.

[189] Cohen, *Individual Security to International Stability*, 10.

Overall, as Janne E. Nolan asserts, cooperative security is like a preventive medicine, while collective security and collective defense are like an acute cure, and they are complementary to each other.[190] The cooperative-security concept has caught on since the end of the Cold War because it has been considered the best way to address the changing needs of global security. This new security environment requires more cooperation, transparency, and collaboration to achieve and maintain stability and peace.

B. COOPERATIVE SECURITY AND NATO- RUSSIAN RELATIONS

Neorealist theory underlines the role of configuration of the international system in relations between states and suggests that interstate relations will be transformed when a change occurs in the configuration. Humanity witnessed this change in late 20th century when the Berlin Wall fell. It "compelled both NATO and Russia to review their approach to one another, the former willing to avoid the re-emergence of the enemy, and the latter wishing not to be isolated from the new international order." [191] From this time on, the cooperative-security concept has provided many opportunities to both NATO and its adversary Russia.

For an era of cooperation and promoting peace and stability in the Euro-Atlantic region, transparency and dialogue are the cure, if not the panacea, whereas uncertainty about the intentions of the adversary, mutual distrust, and cultural differences cause escalation of mutual political anger and constitute the primary obstacles to cooperation. NATO, the most prominent political and security organization of the last half century, has achieved a relatively soft transition from the unstable, bipolar, and realist-minded security environment of the Cold War to a more stable, peace-promoting one by focusing on cures. Particularly in Europe, it has aimed to enlarge its sphere of influence as a peace, democracy, and stability promoter, to the disadvantage of Russia, while trying to avoid offending it. In this regard, its cooperative initiatives since the end of 1960s, particularly after the 1990s, have paid off quite well. Contrary to early USSR–NATO relations

---

[190] Janne E. Nolan, "Global Engagement: Cooperation and Security in the 21st Century." Chap. in *Global Engagement: Cooperation and Security in the 21st Century*. (Washington, D.C.: Brookings Institution, 1994), 5.

[191] Ponsard, *Bridging the Gap*, 128.

between 1949 and 1990, a new period of Russian–NATO relations has been marked by cooperation and dialogue, despite many failures and pitfalls. Holger Mölder points out,

> NATO with the new Strategic Concept approved in the Rome Summit [1991], entered into a new era often called the post-modern society. The creation of North Atlantic Cooperation Council, NATO's first cooperative security arrangement, was the beginning of NATO's new cooperation-oriented security strategy, known as partnership[192]

Mölder offers four models in the post-modern security environment of Europe: security communities, cooperative security arrangements, collective security arrangements, and security complexes.[193] He asserts that cooperative security arrangements are the most effective models for security communities seeking stability and avoiding the emergence of security dilemmas in their neighborhood, because they do not require values sharing and the bonds of treaties while possessing similar guarantees for their defense as members of security communities.[194] Ponsard also claims that the concept of cooperative security does not require commitment from participants beyond a certain level of assurances. It does not require "high institutional mechanisms" such as a membership, or compliance to supranational policies; rather it necessitates close cooperation and preventive action in case of threats to international peace and security.[195]

Mölder thinks that "Cooperative security arrangements that promote interdependence and cooperation have proved themselves as effective measures in order to establish zones of peace, mitigate the possibility for conflicts and avoid the emergence of adversaries." [196] Three main characteristics identified by Molder demonstrate how cooperative security arrangements provide optimum avenues for the relationship between NATO and Russia: first, they are problem-solving oriented, not

---

[192] Holger Mölder, "*NATO's Role in the Post-Modern European Security Environment, Cooperative Security and the Experience of the Baltic Sea Region,*" Baltic Security & Defence Review, Volume 8, 2006, http://www.bdcol.ee/files/docs/bsdr/1-NATO, European Security and the Baltic Sea Region-Holger Molder.pdf.

[193] Ibid., 14.

[194] Ibid., 15.

[195] Ponsard, *Bridging the Gap*, 129.

[196] Ibid., 16.

defense oriented against an aggressor; second, they prioritize common beliefs over common norms, and common norms over common identity; third, they emerge around the security communities. Ultimately, cooperative security arrangements offer NATO "a tailored solution" between maintaining stability and rapid enlargement.[197]

Besides theoretical explanations, historical evidence has also indicated that a cooperative security approach renders the creation of a stable and peace-promoting space in Central and Eastern Europe possible, without leading to major confrontation between the former adversaries. The seeds of a cooperative approach between NATO and Russia were cultivated back in the late 1960s and 1970s. This process, which began with the Harmel Report and culminated in the establishment of the NATO-Russia council, can be identified in three periods: the late Cold War era, post–Cold War era, and post–September 11. During the subsequent four decades in the relationship between Russia and NATO, transparency, cooperation and dialogue have increased, while mutual distrust, antagonism, and differences have decreased.

C.   THE LATE COLD WAR ERA

The quest for dialogue and cooperation to promote peace and stability in Europe dates back to the Harmel Report. Before the Cold War came to an end, "the NATO members had already been working hard to improve security relations in Europe, largely through negotiating arms control and confidence-building measures with the Soviet Union and its Warsaw Pact allies."[198] In late 1960s, the NATO–Russia relations entered a new era called détente. As dialogue intensified between East and West, Western officials began to promote the idea of the establishment of a lasting peace in Euro-Atlantic region via NATO. The "Harmel Report on Future Tasks of Alliance" stressed and accordingly acknowledging the necessity for détente.[199] "Harmel Report reasserted NATO's basic principles and effectively introduced the notion of deterrence and dialogue, setting the

---

[197] Mölder, *Cooperative Security and Baltic Sea,* 17.

[198] Sloan, *Permanent Alliance,* 93.

[199] Ian Q.R. Thomas, *The Promise of Alliance: NATO and the Political Imagination*, Oxford and Lanham, MD: Rowman & Littlefield Publishers, Inc., 1997, 90.

scene for NATO's first steps toward a more cooperative approach to security issues that would emerge in 1991."[200] As Stanley Sloan points out,

> ...particularly after NATO adopted the Harmel Report in 1967, NATO governments actively sought to promote dialogue and cooperation with the Soviet Union and its Warsaw Pact allies. The goal was to try to overcome the East-West division in Europe and prevent the war for which NATO nonetheless continued to prepare.[201]

The Harmel Report requested two functions for NATO: first political and the second military.[202] "It also introduced a new dimension, committing the Alliance to a dual-track policy: it advocated the need to seek a relaxation of East-West relations while maintaining adequate defense . . . ."[203] Yost asserts that "during the Cold War, the Alliance's long-term political objective was rarely expressed more precisely than in the Harmel Report:[204] "The ultimate political purpose of the alliance is to achieve a just and lasting peaceful order in Europe accompanied by appropriate security guarantees."[205] In effect, Harmel Report led to initial cooperative arrangements during the Cold War such as the establishment of CSCE in 1972, talks on mutual and balanced force reductions (MBFR) in 1973, and political ground for intermediate range nuclear forces (INF) in 1985.[206]

The Helsinki final act signed in 1975 "provided the 'rules for the road' for interstate relations in Europe and constructive guidelines for the development of democracy in all European countries."[207] NATO's initiative of détente, the Helsinki Process, resulted in settlement of human rights groups in Eastern Europe that undermined

---

[200] *"The Harmel Report,"* NATO's official site, 12 November 2010, Accessed on 06 June 2012, http://www.nato.int/cps/en/natolive/topics_67927.htm,

[201] Sloan, *Permanent Alliance,* 96.

[202] Thomas, *The Promise of Alliance,* 91.

[203] NATO, *The Harmel Report.*

[204] Yost, *NATO Transformed,* 92.

[205] "The Future Task of the Alliance," report of the Council, annex to the final communique of the ministerial meeting, December 13–14, 1967, par. 9, NATO's official site http://www.nato.int/cps/en/natolive/official_texts_26700.htm.

[206] Sloan, *Permanent Alliance,* 96.

[207] Ibid., 97.

the institutions of Communism and achievement of deals on nuclear and conventional force-reduction treaties in the late 1980s. Sloan for instance points out that "the Conventional Armed Forces in Europe (CFE) treaty of November 19, 1990," a product of this process, "is the most comprehensive, legally binding agreement on conventional arms control ever produced . . . Since the treaty entered into force on November 9, 1992, some 60,000 battle tanks, armored combat vehicles, artillery pieces, attack helicopters, and combat aircraft have been removed from the area and destroyed."[208] All these, attempts, from MBFR, INF to CFE, rendered the military forces of the parties more visible and transparent, and moved them closer to each other.

Eventually, NATO's détente, deterrence, and defense policies contributed to the dissolution of the Warsaw Pact and the disintegration of the Soviet Union in a relatively stable and peaceful way.[209] In sum, it can be argued that the fruits of the process, which began with Harmel Report, the CSCE, MBFR, INF, and the CFE, constituted the preliminary constructive steps for an intensified cooperation and partnership era after the Cold War and contributed significantly to Euro-Atlantic peace and stability by promoting trust, dialogue, and transparency.

D. THE POST–COLD WAR ERA

The end of the Cold War marked the beginning of a new era of major shifts in the Euro-Atlantic security architecture. The predictable status quo of the Cold War was replaced by uncertainty and imbalances in international relations. This new era also created many opportunities for political entities to exist together more peacefully.

The former enemies, Russia and NATO, found themselves in a different security environment accordingly. NATO had long been aspiring to design a space of stability and peace that would enhance democracy and the rule of law in Central and Eastern Europe, from which Soviet influence receded for good a decade before the turn of the millennium. NATO paid particular attention not to offend the former enemy while doing this. Primary inheritor of Soviet Union, Russia, was on the other hand trying to democratize and align

---

[208] Ibid., 98.

[209] Ibid., 96.

itself with the West. It was aspiring to be an equal participant in the new security architecture and did not want to be isolated in Asian steps. As always since Peter the Great, Russia's sanguine feelings about the West suffered from the duality of admiration and hate. It unwillingly admitted the superiority of the West and refrained from alienation. In sum, both NATO and Russia were quite unwilling to see the reemergence of a sort of confrontation that troubled almost a half-century of both of them.

"At Rome," in November 1990, "the Allies loosened the Harmel formula, which had established NATO's dual approach of dialogue and defense, by adding the task of cooperation and partnership with former adversaries."[210] They praised the contributions of the CSCE to peace and stability of Europe and reiterated their determination to create "a new age of confidence, stability, and peace."[211] The North Atlantic Cooperation Council (NACC) in this regard was the first initiative, via which NATO's relations with former adversaries took place until May 1997. NATO took this first formal step immediately after the dissolution of the Warsaw pact, in November 1991.[212] Rome's declaration was inviting former Warsaw pact members to join in "a more structured relationship of consultation and cooperation on political and security issues."[213] NACC was not able to fulfill its mission; however, it provided a formal basis for dialogue in the immediate wake of the fifty-year-old confrontation.

Above all, the NACC was an initiative to prevent the re-emergence of the Cold War division; nonetheless, the limits of it were apparent and well known from its inception. It should be noted that even the step itself was meaningful, considering it was the first concrete arrangement in the beginning of a new era. It provided a formal venue for dialogue, and a rallying point for further cooperative steps. Molder notes "NATO, with the new Strategic Concept approved in the Rome Summit, entered into the new era often called the post-modern society. The creation of the NACC, NATO's first

---

[210] Thomas, *The Promise of Alliance*, 153.

[211] NATO, "The Rome Declaration on Peace and Cooperation," issued by the NAATO Heads of State and Government attending thh meeting of the NAC at Rome, 7–9 November 1991, para. 20, cited in Thomas, *The Promise of Alliance*, 153.

[212] Sloan, *Permanent Alliance*, 100.

[213] "The Rome Declaration on Peace and Cooperation," para.11.

cooperative security arrangement, was the beginning of NATO's new cooperation-oriented security strategy, known as partnership."[214] To Ian R. Thomas "… it allowed NATO as an institution to open bilateral contacts without extending the binding commitment of a security guarantee."[215] It eventually was composed of twenty-two former adversaries in addition to sixteen NATO countries, and served as a forum bringing all NATO members and partners together until Euro-Atlantic Partnership Council (EAPC) replaced it in May 1997.[216]

The Partnership for Peace (PFP), approved in Brussels in January 1994, was another cooperative arrangement that would serve towards the peaceful transformation of Euro-Atlantic security. "The partnership was built on the NACC format and designed to help the alliance and its prospective new members move from the symbols of partnership to the substantive mutual obligations of membership."[217] It has been "a sort of training program for NATO membership" according to a senior U.S. official, as Thomas cited.[218] It has created a venue for countries willing to join NATO to interact with and share knowledge, experience, and expertise. According to Mölder "PfP projects and exercises, and PfP gives non-NATO members access to NATO's military and political bodies, offering a degree of consultation that goes far beyond the dialogue offered by the NACC."[219]

"The PfP has had the required flexibility to cope with an uncertain strategic environment without 'leaving the Russia in the cold," Ponsard asserts.[220] It has been a creative solution to keep Russia oriented towards West, without giving too much

---

[214] Mölder, *Cooperative Security and Baltic Sea*, 18.

[215] Thomas, *The Promise of Alliance*, 156.

[216] Sloan, *Permanent Alliance*, 100.

[217] Thomas, *The Promise of Alliance*, 157.

[218] Ibid., 157.

[219] Alex J. Bellamy, 2004. Security Communities and their Neighbors. Regional Fortresses or Global Integrators? Palgrave MacMillan, 82, cited in Mölder, *Cooperative Security and Baltic Sea.*

[220] Ponsard, *Bridging the Gap*, 67.

authority.[221] It was exactly what NATO officials had been seeking for to outreach former Soviet states, and very valuable for three aspects: First, it gained time; second, no future commitment was made, and third, it did not undermine relations with Russia.[222]

Because PfP has been widely viewed as a preliminary step for membership to NATO, Russians have seen it as an infringement on their security interest and sphere of influence. They have not entirely rejected it in order to maintain ties with the West. Russia, therefore, has chosen to be an "exceptionally passive participant" of the PfP, if civil-emergency planning programs do not count.[223] Even though PfP has not been as fruitful in NATO's relations with Russia as in its relations with other partners, Molder claims that it is "NATO's best-known and most developed cooperative security initiative."[224] From the Russian point of view, it is still a "limited and technical program" that will fail to serve as a basis for the relations between NATO and Russia, no matter how much it has been a useful venue for enhancing military cooperation and reciprocal confidence.[225] Overall, PfP has been an arrangement through which partners promote their security cooperatively, rather than being simply a "waiting room;" and it has provided a communicative framework for constructing common interpretations of norms.[226]

It became clear in the mid-1990s that in addition to others, NATO needed to develop a separate and a special relationship with Russia, which would serve as a basis for improvement of cooperation and development of a lasting partnership. Russia, as well, was willing take such a structural step for improved cooperation. According to Martin A. Smith, two reasons lay behind the requests of Moscow for this special relationship: First it would be viewed as the recognition of Russia's great-power status; second, it would constitute a structural way to participate in the decision-making process

---

[221] Ibid., 66.

[222] Sloan, *Permanent Alliance*, 103.

[223] Yost, *NATO Transformed*, 136.

[224] Mölder, *Cooperative Security and Baltic Sea*, 18.

[225] Ponsard, *Bridging the Gap*, 68.

[226] Mölder, *Cooperative Security and Baltic Sea*, 18.

that would prevent an action not desired by Kremlin.[227] In this regard, the Founding Act, signed in Paris in May 1997 after long negotiations, did meet the first expectation of Moscow, but not the second one. Moscow had to settle for some consultative rights.

The Founding Act was the culmination of the constructive efforts for an enhanced the NATO–Russian cooperation and partnership since the Harmel Report. It introduced the Permanent Joint Council, the first special institution for bilateral the NATO–Russia relations only.

> It marked the beginning of a fundamentally new relationship between NATO and Russia . . . The central objective of the Permanent Joint Council [would] be to build increasing levels of trust, unity of purpose and habits of consultation and cooperation between NATO and Russia.[228]

From the beginning of the negotiations, contrary to Moscow's aim to achieve a venue that would enable it to participate in NATO's decision-making process, NATO's determination to ensure that PJC remained a forum for consultation and cooperation caused tension and delayed a compromise on the framework.[229] Eventually, it was clearly stated in the act that "provisions of this Act do not provide NATO or Russia, in any way, with a right of veto over the actions of the other."[230] Allies denied a greater say of Russia over NATO's actions and decisions. According to Smith "this ensured that Russia could not exploit potential divisions among NATO's members."[231] Even though the PJC did not meet the demands of Russia, it served as a framework and mechanism for consultation and cooperation "to develop common approaches to European security and to political problems."[232]

---

[227] Martin A. Smith, "*NATO–Russia Relations: Will The Future Resemble The Past?*" in, ed. Gülnur Aybet and Rebecca R. Moore, *NATO in Search of a Vision*, (Washington, D.C: Georgetown University Press, 2010), 100.

[228] "Founding Act on Mutual Relations, Cooperation and Security between NATO and the Russian Federation," North Atlantic Council, Paris, 27 May 1997, Preamble, Accessed on 7 June 2012, http://www.nato.int/cps/en/natolive/official_texts_25468.htm .

[229] Sloan, *Permanent Alliance,* 131.

[230] Founding Act, para. 2.

[231] Smith, *Will The Future Resemble The Past,* 101.

[232] Founding Act, para. 1.

Before the first enlargement wave, according to some circles, NATO's move was practically aiming to overcome Russian opposition and any deterioration in relations with a "cooperative embrace," and it was sensible.[233] Peter Trenin-Straussov asserts that Russian leadership, aware of this and cognizant that they could not stall the enlargement process, sought to gain security assurances from NATO that would "minimize the material impact" of the process on Russia's security.[234] In line with this fact, the Allies had to reassure Moscow by reiterating that "they have no intention, no plan, and no reason to deploy nuclear weapons on the territory of new members, nor any need to change any aspect of NATO's nuclear posture or nuclear policy - and do not foresee any future need to do so."[235]

Over all, the Founding Act created the PJC, a distinct venue for the bilateral NATO–Russian relations, granting Russia a unique status, but depriving it of a real say in NATO's internal decision mechanisms. It reassured NATO by reassuring the three-no's regarding deployment of nuclear weapons on the eve of the enlargement process.

Despite the early optimism of both sides, PJC failed to serve effectively as a basis for NATO–Russia relations. Upon NATO's bombing campaign in Kosovo in 1999 without a UN mandate, Kremlin suspended its participation in the PJC, accusing NATO of violating the terms of the founding act.[236] Many commented that PJC failed in its first serious test. However, some, such as Trenin-Straussov, asserted that it had been already apparent that PJC would fail, because "pre-agreed-on positions" of NATO members and their unwillingness to discuss "main political issues" in depth had turned the PJC already into a "talking shop."[237] It was true that it had many defects, but it was an important and effective step in terms of its service as a private dialogue venue for NATO and Russia. The Kosovo Crisis, accordingly, revealed that "serious challenges to Europe's security

---

[233] Sloan, *Permanent Alliance,* 130.

[234] Peter Trenin-Straussov, The NATO–Russia Permanent Joint Council in 1997–1999: Anatomy of a Failure, (Berlin Information-center for Transatlantic Security, BITS Researh Note 99.1 ISSN 1234–3258, July 1999) http://www.bits.de/public/researcnote/m99-1.htm .

[235] Founding Act, para. 4.

[236] Smith, *Will The Future Resemble The Past,* 104.

[237] Trenin-Straussov, *Anatomy of a Failure.*

would likely require significant de facto cooperation, if not full de jure partnership, in order to be tackled effectively besides it led to the suspension of PJC."[238] The NATO–Russia relations did not stall entirely after the Kosovo Crisis and returned to normal after some four months, since both sides were aware of the necessity of cooperation in the new security environment after the Cold War. However, according to Dmitri Trenin, Russia-NATO relations did not fully recover after Kosovo Crisis;[239] it would wait until Putin's ascendance to power in Russia.

E. POST–SEPTEMBER 11 ERA

Major developments in the NATO–Russia relations came after September 11, 2001. Terrorist attacks on U.S. targets revolutionized security concepts and doctrines all around the world, and introduced a new era of cooperation. As an immediate response, two days after the attacks, at PJC's extraordinary meeting, parties pledged to work together and called the entire international community to unite in the struggle against terrorism. During further discussions and meetings in the same year on finding ways to combat terrorism, NATO and Russia decided to forge a new relationship that would serve better for cooperation and working together. Putin's cooperative approach and Tony Blair's encouraging initiative, and later Secretary General Robertson's efforts indicated the consensus over the need for a new cooperative framework. A NATO–Russia joint statement issued on 7 December 2001 at PJC meeting at the level of foreign ministers in Brussels reflected that will:

> Today we commit ourselves to forge a new relationship between NATO Allies and Russia, enhancing our ability to work together in areas of common interest and to stand up to new threats and risks to our security. We reaffirm that a confident and cooperative partnership between the Allies and Russia, based on shared democratic values and the shared commitment to a stable, peaceful and undivided Europe, as enshrined in the NATO–Russia Founding Act, is essential for stability and security in the Euro-Atlantic area. We have decided to give new impetus and substance to our partnership, with the goal of creating a new council

---

[238] Smith, *Will The Future Resemble The Past,* 106.

[239] Dmitri Trenin, "Russia-NATO relations: Time to pick up the pieces," NATO Review vol.48, no. 1, spring 2000, Accessed in June 2012, http://www.nato.int/docu/review/2000/0001-06.htm.

bringing together NATO member states and Russia to identify and pursue opportunities for joint action at 20.[240]

Discussions continued about the details of the arrangement in the first half of the following year. In a conference in February 2002, Secretary General Robertson stated "this conference is another step towards turning a tragedy into an opportunity: A strong relationship befitting NATO and Russia, and benefiting the entire Euro-Atlantic community."[241] Eventually on 28 May 2002 the NATO–Russia Council (NRC) was introduced amid great optimism. The NRC replaced the PJC.

Even though the new council introduced some changes, the overall architecture in fact remained unchanged. According to Lord Robertson, the real difference was "chemistry rather than arithmetic, as even the best format and seating arrangements can be no substitute for genuine political will and open minds on both sides."[242] The NRC would operate on the basis of consensus; decisions would be taken on the basis of equality. This meant that Russia received a co-decision-making right in a council of twenty.[243] All the nineteen areas for cooperation in the founding act remained valid in the context of the NRC. Meetings would be held more regular basis. A preparatory committee was established to prevent "pre-cooked NATO positions" and "19 against 1" situation, which invalidated the NRC for years.

Ponsard asserts "except for the principle of consensus, actually the essential feature of the NRC differing from the PJC's 19+1 format, the NATO Secretary General's chairmanship, and the Preparatory Committee, the functioning of respectively the NRC and the PJC is quite identical."[244] Since the novelties are about main troublers

---

[240] "NATO–Russia Joint Statement," issued on the Occasion of the Meeting of the Permanent Joint Council at the Level of Foreign Ministers in Brussels on 7 December 2001," Press Statement, 7 December 2001, Accessed in June 2012, http://www.nato.int/docu/pr/2001/p011207e.htm.

[241] Lord Robertson, Secretary General NATO, "*NATO–Russia Cooperation in Combating Terrorism: A Good Idea Whose Time Has Come,*" Key note address at the NATO–Russia Conference on the Military Role in Combating Terrorism, 4 February 2002, NATO Defense College, Rome. http://www nato.int/docu/speech/2002/s020204a.htm.

[242] Lord Robertson, "NATO in the 21st Century," Speech at Charles University, Prague, March 21, 2002, cited in Sloan, *Permanent Alliance*, 133.

[243] Smith, *Will The Future Resemble The Past,* 109.

[244] Ponsard, *Bridging the Gap*, 83.

circumscribing the effectiveness of the PJC, the future of the NRC seems brighter than the PJC, in spite of its limitations. The NRC does not grant a veto right that Russians passionately desired, but gives them an equal voice in decisions ranging from counterterrorism to maritime safety. It also provides NATO members a safeguard mechanism by which they could veto any discussion.[245] Overall, the NRC can be considered a balanced and viable solution and a rational venue for increasing partnership and compromise.

Neither the first nor the second huge wave of enlargement gave rise to a confrontation beyond a certain level. However, the missile-defense issue ignited Russian anger. The U.S. decision in 2007 to deploy missile interceptors in Poland and a radar facility in the Czech Republic was the cause of this antagonism. To Stanley Sloan, Russian reaction consists of multiple components. He argues that Russian leadership has been well aware that this planned system does not limit or undermine Moscow's intercontinental ballistic capabilities, and even their viability has not been proven. However, the reason behind their characterization of these systems as a threat inhabits domestic political concerns. The Putin leadership largely devised this argument to consolidate and justify their increasingly authoritarian rule by defining it as a landmark of U.S. influence and power at their front gate. Moscow argued that new NATO missile-defense systems could serve for the purpose of future NATO expansion by threatening Russian missile capabilities.[246]

The NRC's record is not perfect so far, but considering the distance covered since the Harmel Report in 1967, it is satisfactory. In two respects, Martin Smith argues, NRCs record has been relatively impressive: first, unlike the PJC and former efforts, NRC has many institutionalized mechanisms such as a preparatory committee, enabling more equal participation to decision-making and planning processes; second, the scope of activities developed under its auspices is very wide.[247] It seems successful that the NRC was not

---

[245] Smith, *Will The Future Resemble The Past*, 110.

[246] Sloan, *Permanent Alliance*, 141.

[247] Smith, *Will The Future Resemble The Past*, 112.

affected by the Iraq crisis in 2003, during which NATO and Russia embraced opposing policies.[248] In this regard, former Secretary General Robertson asserts that

> ... the existence of the NRC has prevented differences over Iraq from becoming a crisis, like the NATO- Russia Relationship suffered during the Kosovo crisis in 1999. It has brought about a new maturity. It has created a new equality and a new respect for each other, so that we are now capable of disagreeing without falling out . . .[249]

In 2004, during and in the immediate aftermath of the most extensive enlargement wave of NATO, no big deterioration occurred in the NATO–Russia relations. Despite a relatively minor reaction of Moscow, the NRC managed to reconcile Russian reactions. However, NRC has failed in resolving four major issues inherited from the PJC: Kosovo's status, the future of CFE treaty, missile defense, and NATO enlargement.[250]

Overall, the NRC, as the ultimate cooperative security arrangement between former adversaries, is supposed to be considered the latest upgrade of the NATO–Russia relations. Its achievements are more important than its failures in the sense that it is a constructive establishment and its framework for addressing issues is limited and subject to NAC's approval. It is ultimately not a mechanism for problem solving, but rather a forum where all issues can be discussed. Its essential responsibilities were to promote dialogue, mutual understanding, transparency, and practical cooperation, and eliminate distrust and uncertainties.

F.   CONCLUSION

In the wake of the Cold War "the allies faced the challenging task of keeping their commitment to enlarge while avoiding a new confrontational relationship with Moscow."[251]   Cooperative security arrangements have offered NATO "a tailored solution" between maintaining stability in Europe and rapid enlargement in this

---

[248] Ibid.,111.

[249] Lord Robertson , Press conference following the Meeting of the NATO–Russian Council (Brussels:NATO, 2003) http://www.nato.int/docu/speech/2003/s030513a.htm cited in Smith, Will The Future Resemble The Past,111.

[250] Smith, Will The Future Resemble The Past, 113.

[251] Sloan, *Permanent Alliance*, 139.

regard.[252] If we exclude the crises in Bosnia, Kosovo, and Georgia, no high-level confrontation has unfolded between NATO and Russia on a scale of the Cold War. Even though NATO has continued to enlarge its borders and sphere of influence, Russia's reactions mostly remain within the framework of conventional diplomacy and there has been no resort to arms, save in the Caucasus—itself a miracle. The cooperative security concept and its products since the Harmel Report, and especially since 1990, have contributed to peace and stability in the Euro-Atlantic region, prevented a military escalation, and reconciled opposing views by promoting venues dialogue and interdependence. Considering NATO's main concern has been creating a stable and peace-promoting Europe by enlarging its borders and sphere of influence without provoking old enmities with Russia, cooperative-security arrangements have worked well. After all, despite dire predictions by skeptics of the enlargement and transformation of NATO, a fundamental enmity of the most dangerous kind, as in former times, failed to appear.

They served the interest of not only NATO, but also Russia, whose expectations have been to participate in Western security institutions as an equal partner, inhibit decisions that would not be welcomed by the Moscow, and avoid being isolated to Asian steps. The track record of cooperative security arrangements indicates that Russia increasingly gained a greater say in these arrangements, if not a veto power. The arrangements have increasingly become more institutionalized and transparent.

Today the threats to European security are more complicated and transnational.

They include corruption, organized crime, migration, epidemic diseases, environmental catastrophes, and terrorism. For all these reasons, cooperative procedures for enhancing international accountability can be considered the most promising responses to the challenges facing states under the anarchic international system.[253]

Despite many failures and criticism, promoting cooperative security arrangements is the best policy for all parties, since the challenges of the new security environment

---

[252] Mölder, *Cooperative Security and Baltic Sea*, 17.

[253] Ponsard, *Bridging the Gap*, 127.

necessitate more cooperation, transparency, and dialogue. It can be observed that slow and gradual ameliorations created sound partnerships. The more dialogue, cooperation, and interdependence have increased in the NATO–Russia relations, the more the distrust, bias and antagonism have decreased. Over all, a cooperative approach in the NATO–Russia relations has the potential of creating more opportunities and overcoming obstacles in the future, as in the past.

VI. CONCLUSION

For better or worse, the NATO–Russia relations continue to be one of the main pillars of global security architecture in the post–Cold War era, particularly in the Euro-Atlantic region. Stability and peace in Europe and beyond depend on how well the old enemies NATO and Russia design their approaches to each other and construct their relationship on the basis of trust and interdependence. However, the attempts of both sides have remained under a certain level of cooperation, notwithstanding the continual efforts of parties since the Harmel Report in 1967 and the common ground that the new security environment of post–September 11 has prepared for a closer partnership.

"With the end of the Cold War, North Atlantic Treaty Organization (NATO) has continued to struggle to define its identity and clarify its raison d'etre."[254] It sought to create a stable space along the entire Euro-Atlantic region that would be suitable for democracy, rule of law, freedoms, human rights, and liberal economy to flourish. It aimed thus to build partnerships and integrate former Warsaw Pact countries, while trying to avoid a serious confrontation with Russia. Russia, on the other hand, has sought to overcome its economic and sociopolitical imbalances under the influence of nostalgia for the past and promoting its assertiveness in both its traditional sphere of influence and the global stage. In this sense, it considered the enlargement of NATO a threat to its grandiose interests and national security. Moscow's concerns about NATO's goals and strategies have driven it to adopt a reactive attitude from time to time. Relations between the two entities fluctuated between excessive optimism and over-pessimism on the common denominator of distrust. They are wedged between the promise of stronger partnership in an era of unpredictability and transnational threats and lingering memories of old antagonism and distrust.

Since the breakup of the Soviet Union and end of the Cold War, the security environment and threats to security of countries, alliances, and the entire world have changed dramatically. Technological and geopolitical changes revolutionized threat

---

[254] Braun, *NATO–Russia Relations in the Twenty-First Century*, 1.

perceptions and means of reassuring security. The relatively stagnant and predictable nature of the Cold War was replaced by unprecedented uncertainty and unpredictability. Regional ethnic/religious conflicts all around the world, the emergence of transnational terrorist organizations, religious radicalization, the shift in global economic balances, proliferation of weapons of mass destruction (WMDs) and nuclear weapons, and the rising demand for energy and water supplies all pose great risks to global security and peace. This new era of unpredictability and uncertainty has established a common ground for the old enemies Russia and NATO and is gradually bringing them together.

Recently, declarations after the 2012 Chicago Summit, 2010 Lisbon Summits, and recent annual NRC reports and final statements reveal the increasing awareness for the necessity of closer partnership and cooperation, and increasing will in accordance. For instance the final draft of the 2010 Strategic Concept, which was adopted at the Lisbon Summit, formally interprets the desire of the NATO countries to improve constructive relations with Russia and move towards a full-fledged strategic partnership. The recent statements of political leaders and high-level officials from Moscow are in line with these summit reports and declarations. In sum, all strategic concepts, summit declarations, and statements of leaders and top-level officials underline the significance of improvement of the NATO–Russia relations.

NATO's constructive efforts toward security and a resolution of the underlying causes of tension in Europe date back to Harmel Report in 1967, long before the collapse of the Soviet Union. Since then, NATO has sought to normalize its relations with its adversary, limit the escalation of enmity, and end the division of East and West. The Helsinki Act in 1975, North Atlantic Cooperation Council (NACC) in 1990, Partnership for Peace in 1994, Founding Act and Permanent Joint Council in 1997, and finally the NATO–Russia Council in 2002 are the landmarks of the cooperative efforts of NATO before and after the fall of the Berlin Wall.

Russia, on its part, has always been aware of its dilemmas; between economic and structural problems and its grandiose goals, it has sought to align itself gradually with the West in order not to be isolated and to take part in founding the new security systems of post–Cold War and post–September 11. Its responses to NATO's constructive steps, therefore, have been mostly affirmative, if not always.

The major trouble in the post–Cold War era in the NATO–Russian relations, in the view of Moscow, has been the enlargement of NATO. Enlargement of NATO's borders and influence has been read in Moscow as expansion of U.S. influence and strength, filling the vacuum left by the Soviet Union. NATO's extension to Russia's immediate borders naturally has caused concern in Moscow, while paying little heed to the security concern of central and eastern Europeans.[255] However, the amelioration of relations has observed an increasing trend, especially since the advent of the Putin regime in the year 1999, even though it has been slow and gradual and full of frustrations and failures.

There have been several factors leading to ebb and flow in the NATO–Russia relationship. While the traditional insecurity and realist perspectives of Russian leaders and cultural distinction of Russia from the West hinder the advancement of relations beyond a certain level, contemporary geopolitical realities and Russia's long-standing Westernization approaches compel Russia to move closer to the West. Overall, Russia has had to design a balanced foreign policy, which in many respects, favors cooperative, non-confrontational relations with the West and its Asian neighbors, and at the same time, praises its leading role in the former Soviet space and global affairs.

Consequently, Russian foreign policy is the product of the combination of historical, cultural, religious, and geopolitical factors with the rational choices of the Russian elite and people. Along with the legacies of the tsarist and Soviet eras, existing ideological currents among the elites and common people regarding what Russian identity is and how the foreign policy of the Moscow should look effects the foreign policy priorities and designs of the Putin administration.

Russia's foreign policy outlook seemingly changed considerably and become increasingly assertive during the presidencies of Putin and Medvedev. The alleged deterioration of the relations between Russia and the West also has coincided with

---

[255] Sloan, *Permanent Alliance*, 130.

Putin's term in the Kremlin. Many have blamed Putin for the growingly troubled relations between the West and Russia. However, contrary to allegations, Putin's administration has not been responsible for Russia's assertive foreign policy in the 21st century. The change and increasing assertiveness not only started before Putin's rise to office, but are also a product of independent internal and external factors. Moreover, Putin himself has never been anti-Western during his presidency. He is well aware of the need for the modernization of Russia's political and economic systems, and appreciates the achievements in Westernization since Peter the Great. Considering the popular and elite demand for Russia's great-power status and prestigious position in international affairs, it would be nonsense for a political leader to completely ignore such electoral demands. His assertive and sometimes harsh rhetoric against the Western powers makes totally sense and should not lead to conclusions that Putin is anti-Western. Putin basically has sought to maintain its ties and partnerships with the West while trying to avoid ending up subservient in his relations with the West.

This thesis ultimately aims to answer the question of whether a common ground could be constructed between NATO and Russia by analyzing all impeding factors, shared interests, and common challenges that could serve as an inhibitor or catalyst in promoting a strategic partnership. It argues affirmatively that it is possible for Russia and NATO to make a clean sweep of the lingering legacies of deep-seated antagonism and distrust, move beyond cultural, religious, and historical differences between them, and lay the foundations of a healthy, lasting partnership. As Lionel Ponsard argues, "There is still a long way to go before these relations will be fully normalized. However, this past decade of oscillating relations is very instructive in many respects."[256] Common interests and challenges and changing geopolitical dynamics facilitate, and even makes vital, this rapprochement.

Overall, despite many risks and obstacles, the improvement of relations and achievement of a stronger cooperation and true strategic partnership is still possible and important in the NATO–Russia relations, and requires only positive approaches from two

---

[256] Ibid., 2.

entities. There are many opportunities for rebuilding trust and strengthening relations, as well as many impediments. The parties need to concentrate on opportunities and commonalities rather than over-focusing on obstacles and differences, if they are to promote peace and stability in Europe. In this regard, small steps can have a cumulative effect, and the parties should not expect sudden changes and ameliorations. It is particularly important that NATO acknowledge that Russia evolves differently and remain patient during Russia's political evolvement toward democracy. It also has to be ready to recognize a greater say for Russia in its security designs for frictionless, sustainable relations, and a stable and peace-promoting Europe. Cooperative security arrangements offer NATO and Russia a tailored solution between maintaining stability in Europe and their foreign-policy outlooks and improve their partnership and cooperation, gradually. Particularly, the NATO–Russian Council (NRC) looks promising and can continue to serve as a forum for dialogue, which is crucial for the elimination of bias, distrust, and misperception.

THIS PAGE INTENTIONALLY LEFT BLANK

LIST OF REFERENCES

Åslund, Anders. Russia's Surprisingly Liberal New Cabinet. Foreign Policy Magazine. 21 May 2012. http://www.foreignpolicy.com/articles/2012/05/21/russia_s_surprisingly_liberal_new_cabinet.

Arbatov, Alexei G. "Russian National Interests," cited in Mankoff, *The Return of Great Power Politics*.

Bellamy, Alex J. 2004. Security Communities and their Neighbors: Regional Fortresses or Global Integrators? Palgrave MacMillan, 82, cited in Mölder, *Cooperative Security and Baltic Sea*.

Braun, Aurel. *NATO-Russia Relations in the Twenty-First Century*. New York, NY: Routledge, 2008.

Billington, James H. "The Search for a Modern Russian Identity." Bulletin of the American Academy of Arts and Sciences. Vol. 45, No. 4 (Jan.1992). http://www.jstor.org/stable/3824597.

"Bohm, Michael. *5 Reasons Why Russia Will Never Join NATO.*" The Moscow Times. November 19, 2010. Accessed September 16, 2012. http://www.themoscowtimes.com/opinion/article/5-reasons-why-russia-will-never-join-nato/423840.html.

Chicago Summit Declaration. The North Atlantic Council. 20 May 2012.

Cohen, Richard. *Cooperative Security: Individual Security to International Stability*. George C. Marshall European Center for Security Studies, 2001.

Donaldson, Robert H. and Nogee, Joseph L. *The Foreign Policy of Russia: Changing Systems, Enduring Interests*. NY: M.E.Sharpe, April 18, 2009.

Duncan, Peter J S. "Contemporary Russian Identity between East and West." The Historical Journal, 48, (March 2005).

Engelbrekt, Kjell and Nygren, Bertil. *Russia and Europe: Building Bridges, Digging Trenches*. New York, NY: Routledge, 2010.

Erickson, John. "*Russia Will Not Be Trifled with: Geopolitical Facts and Fantasies.*" Journal of Strategic Studies, Volume 22, Issue 2–3, 1999.

"Founding Act on Mutual Relations, Cooperation and Security between NATO and the Russian Federation." North Atlantic Council. Paris, 27 May 1997, Accessed on 7 June 2012. http://www.nato.int/cps/en/natolive/official_texts_25468.htm.

François, Isabelle. "*The United States, Russia, Europe, and Security: How to Address the Unfinished Business of the Post–Cold War Era.*" Center for Transatlantic Security Studies, Institute for National Strategic Studies, NATO Defense University. April 2012. http://www.ndu.edu/inss/docuploaded/CTSS%20Transatlantic%20Perspectives%202.pdf.

Franklin, Simon. "*Identity and Religion.*" In *National Identity in Russian Culture: an Introduction,* edited by Simon Franklin and Emma Widdis Cambridge: Cambridge University Press, 2004 cited in Treeck, Tobias Van. "*Faith in Russia? Exploring National Identity Discourses on Russian Belonging and the Role of Religion.*" Master's Thesis, University of Tampere, 2009.

Friedman, George. "*The Geopolitics of Russia: Permanent Struggle.*" Stratfor, October 15, 2008. http://www.stratfor.com/sample/analysis/geopolitics-russia-permanent-struggle.

———. "*The World in the Next 100 Years.*" 27 August 2009, Accessed 6 November 2012. http://www.newstatesman.com/north-america/2009/08/power-china-world-japan-poland.

"*The Future Task of the Alliance.*" Report of the Council, Annex to the final Communiqué of the Ministerial Meeting. December 13–14, 1967, par. 9, NATO's official site. http://www.nato.int/cps/en/natolive/official_texts_26700.htm.

Graham, Thomas. "*Putin the Sequel.*" American Interest Magazine, Vol. 7, Nu. 4, March/April 2012.

———. "*The Sources of Russia's Insecurity.*" Survival: Global Politics and Strategy, 52:1 (2010): 56. http://dx.doi.org/10.1080/00396331003612471.

Hanson, Philip *et al.* "*Putin Again: Implications for Russia and the West.*" Chatham House Report, February 2012.

"*The Harmel Report.*" 12 November 2010, Accessed 06 June 2012. http://www.nato.int/cps/en/natolive/topics_67927.htm.

How Relevant is Russia to NATO As a Strategic Partner." Senior Course 117, Nato Defense College. January 2011.

Hosking, Geoffrey. *Russia and the Russians: A History.* Cambridge: The Belknap Press of Harvard University Press, 2001. http://www.strategicstudiesinstitute.army.mil/Pubs/display.cfm?pubid=829.

Hyde-Price, Adrian. *"NATO's Political Transformation and International Order."* In NATO's New Strategic Concept: A Comprehensive Assessment, edited by Ringsmose and Sten Rynning, 45–55. Danish Institute for International Studies Report 2011:02.

Inglehart, Ronald. *"Culture and Democracy."* In *Culture Matters,* edited by Lawrence E. Harrison and Samuel P. Huntington. New York: Basic Books, 2000.

Kaczmarski, Marcin. *Domestic Sources of Russia's China Policy.* Problems of Post-Communism, 59(2), Mar/Apr 2012: 3. http://search.proquest.com/docview/1013444519?accountid=12702.

Katsioulis, Christos. *"The New NATO Strategy: A Temporary Compromise."* International Policy Analysis, Friedrich Ebert Foundation, January 2011.

Kelleher, Catherine M. *"Cooperative Security in Europe: New Wine, New Bottles. "* CISSM Working Paper, 13April 2012. Accessed 4 June 2012, http://www.cissm.umd.edu/papers/files/cooperative_security_in_europenew_wine_new_bottles_041312.pdf.

Kuchins, Andrew. "Russian Perspectives on China: Strategic Ambivalence." In The Future of China-Russia Relations, edited by Bellacqua. Cited in Kaczmarski, Marcin. *Domestic Sources of Russia's China Policy.* Problems of Post-Communism, 59(2), Mar/Apr 2012: 3. http://search.proquest.com/docview/1013444519?accountid=12702.

Lavrov, Sergey V. *"Euro-Atlantic: Equal Security for All."* Official Site of The Ministry of Foreign Affairs of the Russian Federation, 24 May 2010. http://www.mid.ru/brp_4.nsf/0/EF1F3C48AD0E5959C325772D0041FA53.

Lo, Bobo. Axis of convenience: Moscow, Beijing, and the New Geopolitics. London, Washington, DC: Brookings Institution Press: 2008. Cited in Kaczmarski, Marcin. *Domestic Sources of Russia's China Policy.* Problems of Post-Communism, 59(2), Mar/Apr 2012: 3. http://search.proquest.com/docview/1013444519?accountid=12702.

Mankoff, Jeffrey. *Russian Foreign Policy: The Return of Great Power Politics.* NY: Rowman & Littlefield Publishers Inc., 2009.

McFaul, Michael. *Between Dictatorship and Democracy.* Washington, D.C.: Carnegie, 2004.

Mölder, Holger. "*NATO's Role in the Post-Modern European Security Environment, Cooperative Security and the Experience of the Baltic Sea Region.*" Baltic Security & Defence Review, Volume 8, 2006. http://www.bdcol.ee/files/docs/bsdr/1-NATO, European Security and the Baltic Sea Region-Holger Molder.pdf.

Moller, Karsten J. "*Russia and NATO after the Lisbon Summit: A New Beginning– Once Again?*" In Nato's New Strategic Concept: A Comprehensive Assessment, edited by Jens Ringsmose and Sten Rynning, DIIS Report 2011.

Monaghan, Andrew. "*From Lisbon to Munich: Russian Views of NATO-Russia Relations.*" Research Report, NATO Defense College, February 2011. http://www.ndc.nato.int/research/series.php?icode=3.

———. Introduction to "*Indivisibility of Security: Russia and Euro-Atlantic Security.*" Forum Paper No.13, 5–25. NATO Defense College, January 2010.

"*NATO's relations with Russia.*" NATO Official Webpage. http://www.nato.int/cps/en/natolive/topics_50090.htm.

"NATO-Russia Joint Statement." Press Statement at Foreign Ministers Meeting of the Permanent Joint Council in Brussels. December 7, 2001. Accessed in June 2012. http://www.nato.int/docu/pr/2001/p011207e.htm.

Nolan, Janne E. "Global Engagement: Cooperation and Security in the 21st century." In *Global Engagement: Cooperation and Security in the 21st century*, edited by Janne E. Nolan. (Washington, D.C: Brookings Institution, 1994).

Ponsard, Lionel. *Russia, NATO and cooperative Security: Bridging the Gap.* London and New York, NY: Routledge, 2007.

Pipes, Richard. *Russia Under the Old Regime.* London: Weidenfeld and Nicolson, 1974.

Putin, Vladimir. Russia and the changing world. RIA Novosti, February 27, 2012.

Rancour, Daniel-Laferriere. *Russian Nationalism From an Interdisciplinary Perspective: Imagining Russia.* New York: The Edwin Mellen Press, 2000.

Robertson, Lord. "NATO in the 21st century." Speech at Charles University, Prague, March 21, 2002, cited in Sloan, Stanley R. *Permanent Alliance? NATO and the Transatlantic Bargain from Truman to Obama.* New York, NY: Continuum, 2010.

———. "*NATO-Russia Cooperation in Combating Terrorism: A Good Idea Whose Time Has Come.*" Key note address at the NATO-Russia Conference on the Military Role in Combating Terrorism. NATO Defence College, Rome, February 4, 2002.

Robertson, Lord. Press Conference following the Meeting of the NATO-Russia Council (Brussels: NATO, 2003). http://www.nato.int/docu/speech/2003/s030513a.htm.

The Rome Declaration on Peace and Cooperation. The North Atlantic Council. November 1991.

"*Russia and the West.*" The Economist, 16 June 2012. http://www.economist.com/node/21556955.

Sakwa, Richard. "Russia's Identity: Between the 'Domestic' and the 'International'." Europe-Asia Studies, 63:6, (2011). http://dx.doi.org/10.1080/09668136.2011.585749.

Shleifer, Andrei and Treisman, Daniel. "A Normal Country." *Foreign Affairs,* Mar/April 2004. Vol. 83, Iss. 2, 20.

Sloan, Stanley R. *Permanent Alliance? NATO and the Transatlantic Bargain from Truman to Obama.* New York, NY: Continuum, 2010.

Smith, Martin A. "*NATO-Russia Relations: Will The Future Resemble The Past?*" edited by Gülnur Aybet and Rebecca R. Moore. *NATO in Search of a Vision.* (Washington, D.C: Georgetown University Press, 2010).

Strategic Concept. The North Atlantic Council. November 7, 1991.

———. The North Atlantic Council. November 20, 2010.

Thomas, Ian Q.R. *The Promise of Alliance: NATO and the Political Imagination.* Oxford and Lanham, MD: Rowman & Littlefield Publishers, Inc., 1997.

Tolz, Vera. "Politicians' Conceptions of the Russian Nation," in *Contemporary Russian Politics: A Reader*, ed. Archie Brown. New York: Oxford University Press, 2001 cited in Duncan, Peter J S. "Contemporary Russian Identity between East and West." The Historical Journal, 48, (March 2005).

———. *Russia: Inventing the Nation.* London and New York: Oxford University Press, 2001 cited in Duncan, Peter J S. "Contemporary Russian Identity between East and West." *The Historical Journal*, 48, (March 2005).

Trenin, Dmitri. "*Russia's Threat Perception and Strategic Posture.*" In Russian Security Strategy under Putin: U.S. and Russian Perspectives. Strategic Studies Institute, U.S. Army War College, November 2007. Accessed September 16, 2012. http://www.strategicstudiesinstitute.army.mil/pdffiles/pub829.pdf.

Torgersen, Dale G. "Kto I Kuda?: Russia, Language, and National Identity." Master's Thesis, Naval Postgraduate School, 2009.

Trenin, Dmitri. *Post-Imperium: a Eurasian story*. Washington, DC: Carnegie Endowment for International Peace, 2011.

———.. "Russia-NATO relations: Time to pick up the pieces." NATO Review Vol.48, No. 1, Spring 2000. Accessed in June 2012. http://www.nato.int/docu/review/2000/0001–06.htm.

Trenin-Straussov, Peter. The NATO-Russia Permanent Joint Council in 1997–1999: Anatomy of a Failure. Berlin Information Center for Transatlantic Security, BITS Researh Note 99.1, ISSN 1234–3258, July 1999. http://www.bits.de/public/researcnote/m99–1.htm .

Tsygankov, Andrei P. "Russia's Foreign Policy." In After Putin's Russia: Past Imperfect Future Uncertain, edited by Stephen K. Wegren and Dale R. Herspring. Lanham, MD, Rowman & Littlefield Publishers, 2009.

Wegren, Stephen K. and Herspring, Dale R. *After Putin's Russia: Past Imperfect, Future Uncertain.* Lanham, MD: Rowman & Littlefield, 2009.

Wittmann, Klauss. *"An Alliance for the 21st century? Reviewing NATO's New Strategic Concept."* In Nato's New Strategic Concept: A Comprehensive Assessment, edited by *Ringsmose and Sten Rynning. Danish Institute for International Studies Report 2011:02.*

Wood, Andrew. *"A Joint Review of the Challenges and Threats of the 21st century."* In Indivisibility of Security: Russia and Euro-Atlantic Security, edited by Andrew Monaghan Forum Paper No.13. NATO Defense College, January 2010.

Yost, David S. *NATO Transformed: The Alliance's New Roles in International Security.* Washington, D.C.: United States Institute of Peace Press, 1998.

Printed in Great Britain
by Amazon